JOHN KEEGAN

THE BATTLE FOR HISTORY

John Keegan was for many years senior lecturer in military history at the Royal Military Academy, Sandhurst, and is now defense editor of the *Daily Telegraph* in London. He is the author or coauthor of ten previous books.

ALSO BY JOHN KEEGAN

A History of Warfare

The Face of Battle

The Nature of War
(WITH JOSEPH DARRACOTT)

World Armies

Who's Who in Military History
(WITH ANDREW WHEATCROFT)

Six Armies in Normandy

Soldiers
(WITH RICHARD HOLMES)

The Mask of Command

The Price of Admiralty

The Second World War

THE BATTLE FOR HISTORY

RE-FIGHTING WORLD WAR II

John Keegan

VINTAGE BOOKS
A Division of Random House, Inc.
New York

First Vintage Books Edition, February 1996

Copyright © 1995 by John Keegan

All rights reserved under International and Pan-American Copyright
Conventions. Published in the United States by Vintage Books,
a division of Random House, Inc., New York. Originally published in
Canada in paperback by Vintage Books, a division of Random House
of Canada Limited, Toronto, in 1995.

Library of Congress Cataloging-in-Publication Data

Keegan, John, 1934–
The battle for history : re-fighting World War Two / John Keegan.
– 1st Vintage Books ed.
p. cm.
ISBN 0-679-76743-6
1. World War, 1939–1945—Historiography. I. Title.
D743.42.K42   1996
940.53'072—dc20   95-24899
CIP

Printed in the United States of America
10 9 8 7 6 5 4 3 2 1

TABLE OF CONTENTS

capitalism, which he loathed, fueled the arsenal of democracy that brought the dictator down. He was a democrat and an English nationalist but believed that his country's best interests would be served by a Soviet rather than an American Alliance, though the United States was the beacon of democracy and the Soviet Union the enemy of democracy at home and abroad. He feared Germany, wished to sustain its postwar division, yet argued that Hitler had stumbled into war in 1939 by miscalculation, not by design. He was always ready to make the strongest moral judgments about men and events but saw history as a chapter of accidents. He was a great historian; however, as such, his chief achievement was to represent the history of the Second World War not as a chronicle of the triumph of good over evil but as a jousting-ground for scholarly dispute. When his now notorious book *The Origins of the Second World War*[1] aroused an almost unanimous denunciation by his peers, he modified his views not at all, reissued it, and added an introduction which reinforced his original argument.

What are the great controversies that surround the war? Some concern its origins, some its conduct, some its personalities, some its mysteries, some its byroads so remote from its central thrust that only specialists regard them as controversial at all. Some controversies are entirely bogus, like David Irving's contention that Hitler's subordinates kept from him the facts of the Final Solution, the extermination of the Jews, or James Bacque's crackpot assertion that Eisenhower was responsible for the deaths

THE BATTLE FOR HISTORY

CHAPTER ONE

CONTROVERSY AND THE SECOND WORLD WAR

"IT WAS A WONDERFUL WAR," wrote A.J.P. Taylor. What war can ever be wonderful, least of all one that killed fifty million people, destroyed swathes of Europe's cultural heritage, devastated its economy, depraved its politics, devalued the very moral basis of its civilization? That, nevertheless, was Taylor's written verdict on the war. He was prepared to repeat his opinion in speech. "What did you feel about the war while it was going on?" I once asked the great historian. "Wonderful," he said. "Wonderful."

Taylor was a notorious controversialist. He hated Hitler, but refused to visit the United States, though its of a million prisoners of war once the war was over. Irving continues to offer a monetary award to anyone who can produce a document authorizing the Final Solution to which Hitler's signature is appended. Bacque, since the publication of the papers of a scholarly conference exploding for good and all the substance of his delusion, has sensibly kept silent.

There may never be a decisive rejoinder to the Taylor thesis that the war came about by accident. His argument, essentially, is that Hitler had won so much advantage by playing on the weakness, irresolution, and disunity of his opponents — over rearmament, the reoccupation of the Rhineland, the annexation of Austria, the dismemberment of Czechoslovakia — that he blinded himself in August 1939 to the possibility of their having a sticking-point. In a progression of diplomatic triumphs, culminating in the Molotov-Ribbentrop Pact, which aborted the chance of squeezing Germany between the military power of Britain, France, and Russia, Hitler may well have seen his aggression against Poland as something that London and Paris would swallow also. To argue otherwise is to claim powers of mind-reading not normally given to humans, let alone historians. We simply do not know how Hitler counted the cards in his hand. We do, however, know what sort of game he was playing. *Mein Kampf* is a significant book; Hitler's speeches to the German people before and after the "seizure of power" are significant also, in the way that the eighteenth-century German philosopher Johann Fichte's *Speeches to the*

German Nation is significant. That famous appeal called
the Germans to nationhood before there was ever a
German state. Hitler's speeches called the Germans to a
new nationhood after the humiliation of defeat, occupation, and what was intended to be permanent disarmament. For Hitler, the First World War had been "the
supreme experience." The defeat of his country devalued
the contribution his generation had made, and the sacri-
fice their parents had made in offering their offspring to
the holocaust of the trenches, and so demanded that the
outcome be put to a second test. "Revenge" does not
quite summarize Hitler's emotions over the war, though
revenge was a powerful ingredient; "readjudication" better describes what he wanted, even at the cost of more
German deaths — to the deaths of non-Germans he was,
of course, perfectly indifferent. He was determined that
Germany should have a victory to expunge Versailles,
thought he could get it by browbeating and outwitting
those who had dictated the Versailles terms, and persisted in that course as far as invading, on September 1,
1939, the former German territory which Versailles had
transferred to the despised Polish state. He expected
Poland to fight, on that no one disagrees. What Taylor
argues is that Hitler did not expect Britain and France to
make good their guarantees to Poland. What almost
everyone says is that Hitler did not care.

  We are dealing with states of mind. Taylor's opponents hold that Hitler's state of mind — violent, vindic-
tive, vengeful — drove German policy to a preordained

war in September 1939. Taylor went to his grave insisting that states of mind are irrelevant in dissecting historical causes. Since state of mind defined everything Taylor did and wrote, which is what made him the pyrotechnician he was, his verdict on the Second World War may be judged his greatest perversity.

There is the making of another controversy afoot about the chief consequence of Hitler's aggression in 1939, the collapse of the Western powers in 1940. For nearly fifty years, the British have taken its outcome for granted: Dunkirk, Churchill's defiant speeches, the Blitz, victory in the Battle of Britain. These were the makings of the national epic, "standing alone," which led eventually to the Grand Alliance and Hitler's overthrow five years later. It has been a major source of national pride for two generations. Now a new generation of historians is beginning to advance the heretical idea that Britain's correct strategy after the fall of France might have been to make peace. Peace was certainly on offer: Hitler was prepared to leave Britain its fleet in return for a free hand on the European continent. The argument has so far had an easy ride. Already, however, there are the rumblings of riposte. Survivors of the Battle of Britain point out that the young simply cannot grasp how "British" Britain was in 1940, how suffused by the sense of British greatness, how contemptuous of foreign mountebanks, how rooted in empire, how certain still that it was the centre of the world. Realists state another case: that any accommodation with Hitler could have been only temporary, that he would have reneged on any deal as soon as he had exploited its advantages, and that the realists of that age, of whom Churchill was one, saw that quite clearly. This is not a controversy that promises to thrive.

A parallel controversy, however, continues to rumble. In June 1940, Britain's ally, France, did arrange an armistice with Hitler, the terms of which left France its fleet and empire. Though, under other terms, northern France was occupied and the French army disbanded, all but for 100 thousand men, the French people generally acquiesced. The successor regime to the Third Republic, *L'Etat français*, led by Marshal Pétain and based at Vichy, engaged their loyalty to a remarkable degree. Most loyal of all were the communists who, until Hitler's attack on Russia in June 1941, were taught by Moscow to denounce resistance to Hitler as the capitalist war. The sole dissident voice was that of de Gaulle, who, on June 18, from London, broadcast his rejection of the armistice and proclaimed the continuing resistance of Free France.

Few joined him at the time. Almost all French men and women were Gaullists by D-Day in 1944. The continuing controversy over Vichy is whether it best served the interests of France in the aftermath of the German blitzkrieg, and up to what point it was honourable for French men and women to offer it their loyalty. In the years after the Second World War, the name of Vichy was execrated and its practice of cooperation with the German occupiers was denounced as treasonable. More recently, as the extent of that cooperation at an individual as well as a state level has come to be recognized, more indulgent views have come to prevail. They have crystallized around the role of the current French president, François Mitterand. Though he eventually rallied to de Gaulle, and acquired an honourable resistance record, he himself now concedes an early involvement with Vichy and admits to the warmth of his personal relationships with several of Pétain's closest collaborators. It seems probable that the eventually objective history of France in the war years will accept practical and working collaboration with the Germans as the experience of the majority of French people for much of the occupation period.

No one more closely collaborated with Hitler in his years of triumph than Stalin. The Russian dictator had made possible the success of the blitzkrieg against Poland and France, by his decision to sponsor the Molotov-Ribbentrop Pact. He greatly profited by its results, which allowed him to annex eastern Poland, incorporate the Baltic states into the Soviet Union, rob Romania and Czechoslovakia of contiguous provinces, and push Russia's boundary almost as far westward as it had been at any time in his country's history. There was a terrible price to pay for his complicity in Hitler's aggression, for the advance to the west had put the Red Army far from its frontier fortifications and spread it out across an indefensible line. When Hitler unleashed his surprise attack on June 22, 1941, the Soviet forces collapsed immediately. Stalin himself was stunned by the onslaught and underwent something like a nervous breakdown, which robbed him of the power of command during the first weeks of the campaign. Had he been the victim of self-delusion in the months before Operation Barbarossa? The signs of a gathering German offensive were there to see for those who would look. Hitler had been transferring his attack divisions eastward for nearly a year. The British, through Sir Stafford Cripps, issued their first warning to the Russians of their suspicion that Hitler was planning Barbarossa on June 14, 1940, a year and eight days before its start. Thereafter, information from many sources — intercepts of Japanese diplomatic traffic, Swedish and Czech assessments, American appreciations — filtered through to Moscow. On April 3, Winston Churchill himself pointed out to Stalin in a personal message that armoured divisions used in the blitzkrieg on Yugoslavia had been transferred to Poland, ending: "Your Excellency [Stalin] will readily appreciate the significance of these facts." Stalin chose to ignore all such warnings. He even made acceptance of Hitler's friendly intentions a sort of loyalty test among his intimates and in the high command. The consequences for his Soviet fellow citizens were catastrophic. Information drawn from the opening of the Soviet archives suggests that as many as forty-five million may have died as a result of the German aggression, not twenty million as previously thought, and the reasons for Stalin's determination not to take adequate precaution against the probability of a German attack will fuel controversy over the Stalinist dictatorship for years to come.

An older controversy surrounds the origins of another surprise attack, that on Pearl Harbor by the Japanese on December 7, 1941. The result of that attack was the sinking or disabling of most of the battleships of the U.S. Pacific Fleet at their moorings, though — fortunately — not of the aircraft-carriers, which happened to be at sea. Many authors, and an official enquiry, have explored the question of why surprise was possible on such a scale. There have also been explorations of the allegation that Roosevelt had foreknowledge but chose not to act on it, as a means of bringing the United States into the Second World War on the anti-Axis side. Objective analysis seems successfully to support the view that Japanese security and deception measures were elaborate enough to disguise the movements of the Combined Fleet until it was in its attack positions; in light of a certain weariness and routinism by the U.S. Pacific Fleet in its response to repeated calls to high readiness, such measures appear to dispose of suggestions that Roosevelt might have known of an impending attack. More recently, however, the allegations have taken the new twist that Churchill, through his national decryption system, enjoyed foreknowledge but declined to pass it on to Washington precisely because he knew that a surprise attack would bring the United States into the war on Britain's side, a development he had been seeking to arrange since Dunkirk. Conspiracy theorists allege that the British intelligence archives, if and when opened, will reveal that to be the truth. Two caveats may be entered: one is that, since

American decryption of Japanese ciphers was superior to British efforts, it is unlikely Washington lacked knowledge that London had; the other is that Japanese treachery by no means guaranteed an American declaration of war on Hitler. Indeed, Pearl Harbor so outraged the United States that it is perfectly possible popular emotion might have forced Roosevelt to deploy American forces to the Pacific *en bloc*, leaving Britain as isolated as before. What averted that eventuality was Hitler's quixotic decision, four days after Pearl Harbor, to declare war on the United States, something he was under no obligation to do.

Why did Churchill, in another theatre of war, also act quixotically, to Britain's great disadvantage in the conduct of operations? In that theatre — Greece and the eastern Mediterranean — perhaps the boldest strategic stroke of the war was to transfer what remained of British striking power to the Middle East, even while the home islands lay under threat of invasion. The deployment brought the first victories of the war, in the Western Desert and then East Africa. Those further humiliations of Mussolini, who had already faced the repulse of his invasion of Greece in October 1940, prompted Hitler to send Rommel and the Afrika Korps to Libya. Before that intervention, however, Churchill had diverted parts of the Western Desert Force to Greece, to stiffen its resistance to the Axis, and he further reinforced Greece in the early months of 1941 on receipt of intelligence that Hitler was planning an offensive into the Balkans, and perhaps into Turkey. The outcome was disastrous for Britain on several fronts. The German invasion of Yugoslavia in April immediately led to an invasion of Greece, during which the British Expeditionary Force was overwhelmed. The absence of that force from the Western Desert facilitated the first of Rommel's successful offensives from Libya into Egypt. The British evacuation of its troops from Greece to Crete exposed them to defeat by a German airborne invasion, the strategic and tactical brilliance of which even the British conceded.

Why did Churchill allow Hitler these advantages? There seem to have been two reasons, one political and justifiable, one military and hollow. Churchill sent troops to Greece because the Greeks, with the Yugoslavs, were the only unconquered peoples on the European continent who were prepared to make common cause with the British in standing up to Hitler. The Yugoslavs he was unable to help; time lacked and geography was against an expedition. Greece, by contrast, was accessible and robustly anti-Axis. Churchill seems to have taken the view that, however dubious the prospect of success, British credibility as an enemy of Nazism depended on supporting friends whenever they could be reached. That was the political justification, and it still looks good. The military reason was less well-founded. Churchill, perhaps because of his championship of the Gallipoli campaign in 1915, entertained an exaggerated opinion of the military importance of the eastern Mediterranean and Turkey. He saw the region as a key to strategic control of Germany's and Russia's southern flank, and Turkey as a potentially powerful ally in his war against the German enemy.

In the long run, British intervention in the Balkans did achieve the political objects Churchill pursued. The Greeks did come to trust in British friendship; did accept its intervention in 1944, which ensured the defeat of the Communist partisans, as well-intentioned; were brought by it firmly within the Western Alliance, which, in retrospect, may be seen as a crucial event in denying Stalin's Russia any Mediterranean foothold during the Cold War. More indirectly, Churchill's support of Tito, the successful party in the Yugoslav civil war, served the same ends. His readiness to break with Stalin in 1948 may be traced back to British support of his version of the Yugoslav nationalism in 1943–44. By contrast, the expectation that Turkey might be brought into the war on Britain's side looks increasingly to have been a chimera, one of those strategic fantasies to which Churchill, as his chief of staff, Alanbrooke, continuously complained, was temperamentally prone. The climax of Churchill's Mediterranean obsession came in the autumn of 1943, when against strong and wise American advice, he committed British troops to the occupation of the Ionian islands off the Turkish coast, an operation conceived in the belief that it would push the Turks into cobelligerency with the West. The Americans warned that German air superiority in the region would lead to disaster, as it did. Diplomatic opinion, subsequently validated, was that Turkish foreign policy in the war years had but a single object, which was to protect Turkish interests by the avoidance of taking sides. Turkey may be regarded as the most successful neutral of the Second World War.

The United States, traditionally committed to direct rather than indirect strategy as a means of winning wars, had little sympathy with the intricacies of Mediterranean operations. Its wish, from 1942 onwards, was to organize a major assault on Hitler's Europe as soon as possible and by the most direct route, via northern France. In the spring of 1942, it sent a mission to London to urge an invasion that year. The British realistically demonstrated that such an enterprise would fail. The Americans then proposed that it should be staged in 1943. To that, the British were opposed also, and they got their way. The vanguard of the great army gathering in the United States was shipped to North Africa for the Operation Torch landings, which led, against growing American reluctance, to the Sicilian and Italian campaigns. The British view traditionally has been that there was no other way, and that the Mediterranean profitably occupied the Allied force until preparations which defied abbreviation could be completed for the cross-Channel invasion in 1944. There are dissentient voices. Germany, it is said, was actually weaker in 1943 than in 1944, more embroiled on the Russian Front, shorter of first-class equipment like the Tiger tank. The Atlantic Wall had not been completed; the German divisions in France were under-strength and underequipped. There is a great deal in this. Moreover, with hindsight, we know that Hitler had undergone a severe crisis of confidence after his defeat at Stalingrad, allowing his chief of staff, Zeitzler, to take the initiative in strategic planning and so launch what proved to be the disastrous Kursk endeavour. Had the Allies in the west been ready to invade France while the Kursk battle was at its height in July 1943, it is not impossible that it might have succeeded. Hindsight is the condition, however, which must be stressed in making that judgment. A cross-Channel invasion staged in 1943 would have had to be prepared in 1942. In that year, the Battle of the Atlantic had not been won, the strategic-bombing offensive against German cities was only beginning, the base for a great American army in Britain had not been built, the landing fleet was still under construction, and so on. Germany may well have been less ready to withstand an Allied cross-Channel invasion in 1943 than it proved to be in 1944; but Britain and America were less ready to mount it. The controversy seems pointless.

Allied to this controversy is another over the role of the resistance. Enthusiasts for the potentiality of "low-intensity warfare," the sort of popular guerrilla campaigning which so badly troubled the dissolving European empires in Africa and Asia after 1945, have argued that, had the resistance in France, Scandinavia, and the Low Countries been supplied with adequate equipment, it might have created conditions akin to those prevailing in Yugoslavia in 1943–44 and so opened an internal "Second Front," which would have weakened the German occupation forces to a point where a cross-Channel invasion would have succeeded much more easily than it did. Here, hindsight is merely misleading. Imperial forces failed against guerrillas in the wars of decolonization because they were fought under the scrutiny of the world press; it might also be said that they failed because the retreating empires felt bound by a moral code that Nazism both violated and despised. There was no foreign press to scrutinize Hitler's occupation forces, and they obeyed the simple code that defiance would be punished by massacre, deportation, and the extermination camp. In Yugoslavia, geography hampered their efforts to visit fire and sword to every dissident region; in France, which offered guerrillas few refuges, the attempts to create "liberated areas" at Vercors and Glières brought insensate reprisal. The Germans simply killed everyone they could catch — men, women, and children, indiscriminately. The notion that the resistance had a potentiality to open the way for a conventional invasion by regular forces of the Anglo-American alliance is, therefore, wishful thinking. Anyone who entertains it should recall that Yugoslavia, the one German-occupied country to mount a nationwide guerrilla campaign, lost no fewer than 10 per cent of the population as a consequence.

The sufferings of the European people under Hitler's rule will be the subject of controversy for generations to come. All who actively opposed Hitler suffered. So, as we know, did people who offered no resistance at all, notably the Jews. Under the Nuremberg laws, the Nazis had succeeded in forcing many German Jews to emigrate from the Reich before the war of 1939 broke out. Their policy was to make the German lands *judenrein*, clean of Jews. When their conquests made them masters of new lands containing communities of German Jewish refugees, as in France, and of much larger communities of historically settled Jews, particularly in Poland, Belorussia, and the Baltic states, they changed their policy. Since there was, after the breach of diplomatic relations with the outside world, nowhere to which the Jews might be expelled, they decided on a "Final Solution of the Jewish Problem." By a decision taken at Wannsee, a suburb of Berlin, in January 1942, the Jews within the Nazi area of control were simply to be killed, and a fixed method was settled upon. Extermination camps were set up in remote areas of Poland, to which Jews were to be transported as if cattle, and there gassed to death in hundreds of thousands.

This, both the most shameful and most extensive exercise in massacre in human history, far exceeding the atrocities of Genghis Khan or Tamerlane in scale, has excited justifiable controversy to this day. What did the Allies know? What could they have done to stop it? That the Allies did know something of the extent of the massacre seems undoubted; some who escaped from the extermination camps brought word of the horror to the West. Despite that, the Allies notably dragged their feet over offering refuge to small parties of Jews as managed to escape the Nazi net. Some perished on the journey;

some were thrown back into the hands of the killers. None of that is defensible. The record, however, raises a larger question: why did the Allies not destroy the Nazi means of human destruction? In particular, why did they not bomb Auschwitz, the camp in Polish Silesia at which more Jews — and hundreds of thousands of non-Jews — were massacred than in any other place? Nearly two million Jews were killed at Auschwitz. It was a large place and presented a large target. The emotional argument seems overwhelming.

Emotion, of course, is misleading. Bombing Auschwitz would simply have assisted the Nazi work of massacre; one of the greatest horrors of the Second World War is that bombing — in both Germany and Japan — did kill thousands of innocents confined in camps near other targets. Choosing Auschwitz as a target would have added to that toll. Why then, the more sophisticated argument runs, did the Allies not bomb the railways that fed Auschwitz? The rail network to Auschwitz-Birkenau, the chief killing place, is extensive; I have walked over its rusting tracks.

That failure is more difficult to explain away. Bombing the railways would certainly have interrupted the massacre. It would, however, only have interrupted it. The damage would have been repaired, perhaps using the labour of those inside the camp awaiting their death. Repetition of the damage would have been repaired by the same means. The irony is ghastly. Auschwitz had the capacity to be a self-sustaining killing machine, until the site itself was captured by Allied forces, as it was by the Russians in January 1945. Bombing, one of the principal means by which the Allies sought to defeat Nazism, was almost powerless to check the worst of Nazi criminality.

The defectiveness of bombing as a means of curtailing Nazi atrocity introduces the general question of its utility — and so, of its morality — as a means of waging war. At the outbreak in 1939, all the combatant powers, Germany as well as France and Britain, forswore the bombing of civilian targets. Then, in May 1940, the Germans bombed by mistake the German city of Freiburg im Bireisgau and, to disguise the error, blamed it on the enemy. Thereafter, it was open season. On September 7, 1940, once it had become clear to the Germans that they could not defeat the Royal Air Force in the skies during what Churchill had already called "the Battle of Britain," they launched their bomber waves against London and burnt out the East End. Britain retaliated, perfectly ineffectively. During 1941, more RAF aircrew were killed in flights to German targets than Germans in the target areas. In 1942, Britain decided on a change of policy. A new chief of Bomber Command, Arthur Harris, decided to abandon precision bombing of military targets and to "dehouse" the German civilian population of the great industrial cities. The object was disorganization and demoralization. More accurately, the Germans called it "terror bombing." Terror bombing, "area bombing" to the RAF, continued until the end of the war. The U.S. Army Air Force, after its arrival in mid-1942, essayed precision bombing for some time but, after the defeat of its early raids on high-value targets, effectively adopted area bombing as well.

It did not work. Defenders of the campaign argue otherwise, but the objective analysis is that, though bombing did, in the last months of the war, halt the German production of essentials such as synthetic oil and close down movement on Germany's railways and inland waterways, the effect cannot be separated from that produced by the advance of the Allied ground armies from east and west. By the spring of 1945, when the bombing force rode the skies of Germany unopposed and bombed where they would, as at Dresden, the German army was a spent force, unable to oppose the onward march of the Red and Anglo-American armies and already foredoomed to defeat. That was the verdict which Hitler himself accepted and which drove him to choose suicide.

Bombing unquestionably, by contrast, brought about the defeat of Japan. By July 1945, when American land and sea forces were still hundreds of miles from the Japanese home islands, the American air forces had burnt out 60 per cent of the ground area of Japan's sixty largest cities, and the country hovered on the brink of economic collapse. Two million people were employed digging up the roots of pine trees, from which a primitive form of aviation fuel could be distilled; the fleet had no fuel for offensive missions, and inter-island ferry traffic had been halted by American submarines, which roamed the inland sea at will. A rational government would have conceded defeat. The country was on the brink of starvation. Disaster stared it in the face. "Face," however, in the Japanese sense, prevented it from accepting reality. Then, in August, two new crises offered the Emperor and his military cabinet a way out. On August 6, an American aircraft dropped an atomic bomb on the city of Hiroshima. On August 8, the Red Army invaded Manchuria. The Manchurian campaign was victoriously concluded on August 17, eight days after the second atomic bomb had been dropped on Nagasaki and two days after the Japanese had surrendered to the United States.

Hence, the last controversy of the Second World War: did Japan give in because it feared a third atomic bombing? Or did the total defeat of its largest army, the garrison of Manchuria, show it that further resistance was impossible? Rationally, there seems little to dispute the efficacy of the atomic bomb as the means which brought the Second World War to an end; it was that which Emperor Hirohito invoked as the explanation for surrender before any foreign soldier had set foot on Japanese soil. Historians, however, are committed to controversy as a way of life, and this controversy may never be settled.

It may, moreover, not be the last controversy. In a Europe divided by the challenge of federalism, the lines are drawn between those who see the European Union as a triumph of idealism and supranationalism and those who see it as "Germanization by other means." The most extreme opponents of union point to its preconditions — a single currency, a common agricultural policy, economic convergence — as those the Nazi regime laid down for its "European Economic Community" in January 1942. The problem of Germany has been at the root of Europe's troubles since 1871. Controversies over the causes and nature of the Second World War illuminate but do not dispose of it.

CHAPTER TWO

HISTORIES OF THE
SECOND WORLD WAR

THE HISTORY OF the Second World War has not yet been written. Perhaps in the next century it will be. Today, though fifty years have elapsed since it ended, the passions it aroused still run too high, the wounds it inflicted still cut too deep, and the unresolved problems it left still bulk too large for any one historian to strike an objective balance. That should not surprise us. Not until 1988 did an American historian, James McPherson, succeed in publishing a one-volume history of the American Civil War that 130 years after the conflict's conclusion, generally satisfied all shades of historical opinion over its causes, nature, and consequences.[1] Moreover, that conflict concerned only one nation, and its history add-ressed a society transformed by an intervening century.

The Second World War involved as participants every state existing in the world in 1939, with the exception of Sweden, Switzerland, Portugal, Spain, the Irish Free State, Iceland, Greenland, Afghanistan, Tibet, Mongolia, and Yemen. Even Turkey, the most diplomatically prudent of European states, declared war on Germany on March 1, 1945; even Argentina, least anti-Axis of South American states, declared war on Japan on February 8. Portugal, Iceland, Greenland, moreover, were more or less willingly implicated in 1941–42 by their provision of bases to the Anglo-American alliance, while Sweden's industrial output was perforce harnessed to Germany's after the fall of Denmark and Norway in April 1940. Perhaps, only among states adjacent to the theatres of conflict, only Switzerland, whose disinvolvement was useful to both great opposed coalitions, Ireland, and Spain may be regarded as true neutrals. Irish and Spanish neutrality, in any case, was determined by their common and recent experience of civil war. The Second World War was truly a world war, involving all existing states and empires; only those too utterly remote to participate or too harshly marked by recent internal wars of their own making remained aloof.

Any history of the Second World War is, therefore, a history of the world between 1939 and 1945. Yet, it must be more than that. For China and Japan alike, the war that became the Second World War began, perhaps, in

1931, when Manchuria passed from Chinese to Japanese administration, and certainly in 1937, when the Japanese army embarked on its conquest of the Chinese littoral. For Greece, which succeeded in avoiding involvement in the European conflict until April 1941, the war persisted until 1947, when the last centres of Communist insurrection were extinguished at the end of a civil war that had engulfed the country since the German departure in 1944. In Indo-China, which fell under Japanese occupation in 1941, the capitulation of August 1945 did not bring peace. The Vietnamese nationalists resisted the reimposition of French rule, initiating a war that did not end until 1955, was resumed again in the 1960s, and perhaps persists to this day.

Thus, the history of the Second World War not only has no spatial limits, but also escapes neat or easy positioning in time. Did it begin in 1939, or in 1931? Did it end in 1945, or 1947, or 1955? Is it really over at all? The last question is given particular force by the apparently unresolvable conflict in Yugoslavia, the roots of which are all too clearly traceable to the destabilization of that country by the partisan war of 1941–44. All wars, of course, leave a residue of unresolved issues behind them. Indeed, the Second World War may itself be seen as the direct outcome of issues left unresolved by the First World War, raising for the historian the challenge of writing a satisfactory account not simply of five, but perhaps of thirty, years of world history, from the crisis of 1914 to the unconditional surrenders of 1945. Such a history, moreover, might be no more than the first volume of two, the second being necessarily devoted to chronicling the mistrust, misunderstanding, and competition between the victors of 1945 in the forty-five years of the Cold War that followed their apparently conclusive triumph.

Writing the history of the Second World War will not, therefore, be any straightforward task. Nor have the tentative efforts made so far proved simple or uncontroversial. I know that from my own experience, not as the author of a Second World War history for whose comprehensiveness I would make very modest claims, but as a child of the war who was caught up in its drama, followed its course with passionate interest, read voraciously among the early historical accounts, and continued to follow its developing historiography into and subsequently throughout his adult life. By now, fifty years after 1945, I have read very extensively indeed. There are few aspects of the war about which I do not know something, and several about which I know a great deal. Nevertheless, it is the limitation rather than the scope of my knowledge of which I am most aware. In what will follow, therefore, I attempt no vision of what an eventual history of the Second World War ought to be. On the contrary, I present one historian's record of his exploration of the literature so far, singling out in particular two sorts of books: those I have read because I thought them essential to an understanding of the war, and those which, for one reason or another, including vividness of style, depth of sensibility, or particularity of approach, illuminate understanding. These categories of course, will in some cases overlap.

They do so in the first book I select for notice — *The Struggle for Europe,* published by New Zealand war correspondent Chester Wilmot in 1951.[2] The scheme of arrangement I have chosen for this short and personal study divides the written history of the war into five categories: (a) general, including official, histories; (b) biographies; (c) campaign histories; (d) treatment of special subjects, including intelligence, economic warfare, and technology; and (e) civilian histories, particularly of occupation, resistance, and genocide. Chester Wilmot's book is remarkable because it comprehends several of these subjects in a single volume. However, it is also remarkable in many other ways.

It is remarkable to me because it opened my eyes to a way of writing the history of the Second World War which was not simply an essay in triumphalism. I was born in 1934, and so was eleven years old when the war ended. It had dominated my early life, and therefore my most formative years. My earliest memory of an experience outside the domestic routine is of evacuation from London to the countryside during the Munich crisis of September 1938; my last memory of the events of the war is of grown-up crossness at the celebration, by myself and some friends, of the end of the fighting in the Pacific just a few days before the official announcement of the Japanese surrender in August 1945. In the intervening seven years, my grasp of the war's unfolding had been largely formed by a series of official short histories published by her Majesty's Stationery Office, some of which I still possess. As official wartime histories go, these pamphlets still seem to me models of objectivity. While putting the best face on things, they tell no lies and admit a good deal of the truth. By their nature, however, they necessarily conceal all hints of dispute over strategy or tactics within the British direction of the war, any mention of personal incompetence, and all reference to inter-Allied differences.

Chester Wilmot changed all that, not only for me, but for the vast Anglo-Saxon readership of the war's history. In the five years after the war's end, he had devoured the sources thus far published, including the forty-two parts of the Nuremberg Trials documents and the *U.S. Strategic Bombing Survey*, and formed a view of the way the war in the West had been fought which exploded for good the received version — the Churchillian version of resolution, defiance, victory, and peace, which the great war leader began to develop in the six volumes of his history that appeared from 1948 onwards.[3] He revealed the existence of Anglo-American differences over the location, scale, and, above all, timing of the invasion of Northwest Europe. He disclosed, though perhaps rather exaggerated, the differences between Eisenhower and Montgomery over the conduct of the campaign once the landings were successfully mounted in 1944. He identified the extent of the extraordinary German recovery in the autumn of 1944, when the Wehrmacht appeared to be on the verge of collapse. Controversially, and perhaps wrongly, he attributed the fall of Eastern Europe to Stalin to Allied strategic indecision during the development of the liberation campaign, thus helping to determine, even initiate, the great postwar debate over the origins of the Cold War.

For me, he did much more. He showed me how military history should be written. *The Struggle for Europe* remains, in my estimation, a revolutionary book in which are combined, as I believe had not been done before, not only strategic commentary and historical narrative, but penetrating economic and operational analysis, character portraiture, and, above all, riveting tactical description. Wilmot turned himself into a historian to write *The Struggle for Europe*, a historian of formidable quality; but he had been a war correspondent, and the events he described he had often witnessed at close hand or heard about soon afterwards by direct questioning of participants. He belonged to the new school of war reporting, in which the reporter saw his task as one to be discharged as much on the front lines as at headquarters, and he was among the foremost practitioners of the new approach. Oddly, he was a loner among his fellows, admired but not much liked, aloof and abrasive. It may well have been those qualities which fitted him to write his extraordinary book. It had no successor. In 1954, three years after its publication, by which time he was one of the best-known journalists in the world, he was killed in the crash of the original Comet jet airliner over the Mediterranean.

Yet, though he wrote only one book, it was enough, at least for me. He had depicted how military history in general, that of the Second World War in particular, might, and perhaps ought to be, written: rigorously but vigorously, with emotional passion but intellectual dispassion, from the widest possible perspective and variety of sources and never, never without remembrance that the drama of war is a tragedy for those touched by its fatal consequences.

How many large treatments of the Second World War pass those tests? Wilmot's history is not comprehensive. It concerns, as its title makes clear, the war in Europe, and on the Western Front in particular. It has little to say of the ghastly war in the east, and almost nothing about the war in Asia and the Pacific. Few authors have attempted serious one-volume narratives, and none is wholly satisfactory. Guy Wint and Peter Calvocoressi's *Total War*, though rightly admired for its inclusiveness, does not yield on close inspection those detailed explanations of operational causes and consequences which a military history ought to provide.[4] Gerhard Weinberg's recent *A World at Arms* is encyclopaedic in its coverage of sources and of the war's events, military and non-military, in every sector, but is curiously bloodless; the author lacks, as Wilmot did not, the gift of communicating the thrill and horror of combat, which is the core of war experience.[5] Martin Gilbert's *Second World War* is a strange book.[6] As the official biographer of Churchill, he has an unrivalled knowledge of the conduct of the war by the British and the Anglo-American high command; nevertheless, his self-confessed dedication to the establishment of strict chronology imposes a jerky, scrapbook quality on his writing which robs his narrative of fluency. We all recognize the play of chance in human affairs, what academic jargon calls "the stochastic element;" however, what elevates state war-making over that of the primitive world is the pursuit of strategic objects, which, though it may fail, nevertheless has a history of its own, separate from, if constantly affected by, day-to-day eventuality. Gilbert's method is a warning that attention to chronology, though essential to the historian, can be distortive as well as corrective.

I have not yet begun to read the German official history of the war, *Das Deutsche Reich und der Zweite Weltkrieg*, whose first volumes are now appearing in English, though I have discussed its composition with some of the historians working on it at Freiburg.[7] The British official history, *History of the Second World War, HMSO*, divided into a civil and a military series, is now complete. It is an admirable achievement, within the limitations of traditional official-history writing, initiated by the General Staff in Germany in the nineteenth century. Few volumes stand out. In the civil series, one of them is *Design and Development of Weapons*, whose three authors include the distinguished historian of the medieval period M.M. Postan.[8] Though writing on what must have been to him the alien subject of aircraft manufacture, he brilliantly conveys the difficulty encountered by a second-rank economy in competing at the forefront of technology in what, for much of the time under review, was literally a life-and-death struggle for national survival. Among the many volumes of the military series, though they combine to provide a complete history of the British services at war, few of the authors shine. The series is overweighted towards the Mediterranean and Middle East, a criticism reflected in American opinion of British strategic preoccupations, and there is a tenderness for reputations, which, though not as marked as in the obsequious volumes of the official history of military operations of the First World War, deprives the narratives of bite. The explanation of the tone derives from the origins of the authors: most were retired regular officers, such as Captain S.W. Roskill, the author of the three-volume *The War at Sea*, or themselves participants, like Noble Frankland, the joint author with Sir Charles Webster of the history of British strategic bombing.[9]

American official history is in a different and superior class altogether. The United States had undertaken no full-scale official narration of its part in the First World War at all, unlike the other victors, or indeed the vanquished: both Germany and Austria, if not Turkey, have memorialized the Great War at exhaustive length. At the outset of its involvement in the Second World War, the United States decided on a revolutionary approach to the business of recording a national military experience. It recruited a contingent of young and not so young academic historians and authorized them to accompany

military, naval, and air units into the field, with the
object of accumulating "after-action reports" in the
immediate aftermath of combat. Not always the aftermath: Forrest Pogue, one of the authors of the volumes
on the North-West Europe campaign, was at Omaha
Beach on June 6, 1944, and debriefed wounded survivors
in hospital ships offshore that evening, as I heard him
describe to President Clinton in the White House, at a
Second World War Commemoration dinner almost fifty
years later to the day.[10]

The U.S. Army series of official histories is a stupen-
dous achievement, which comprehends not only carefully
periodized volumes for each campaign, no fewer than six
— Harrison's *Cross-Channel Attack*, Blumenson's
Breakout and Pursuit, Cole's *The Lorraine Campaign* and
The Ardennes, and Macdonald's *The Siegfried Line
Campaign* and *The Last Offensive* — for that of North-
west Europe, 1944–45, but also high-level, strategic studies, such as Pogue's *Supreme Command*, and monographs
on such specialized topics as the rearmament of the Free
French forces from American stocks.[11] The ground cov-
ered by the official histories of Northwest Europe has
been brilliantly comprehended by Russell Weigley in
Eisenhower's Lieutenants, a book which bears compari-
son with its eponym, Douglas Southall Freeman's *Lee's
Lieutenants*.[12]

The campaigns fought by the U.S. Army Air Forces
are comprehensively, if rather dutifully, related in a series
of official volumes by W. Craven and J. Cate that follow

the traditional style of operational history established in Europe before and after the First World War.[13] In a class quite by itself is the naval series, directed and, in quite large part, written by the formidable Samuel Eliot Morison. Morison, a Harvard professor, historian of the discovery of North America and much else, and an intrepid small-boat sailor in his own right, was raised to the rank of admiral by a grateful U.S. Navy, for reasons which the scope and quality of his enterprise amply reveal. Its fifteen volumes succeed not only as narrative and analysis but often also as literature. Morison's account of the Battle of Midway, not only the turning-point of the Pacific War but an almost uniquely dramatic event in the annals of warfare, is a brilliant and memorable piece of writing.[14]

The history of the war on the Russian front, which in the long view will undoubtedly come to be seen as the central event of the Second World War, remains the least well recorded of all its episodes. The Soviet official history was translated into German by the East German government but, as an exercise in Marxist historiography, has been found of little use by Western historians. An approximation to a satisfactory, official history exists in the two volumes written by the British historian John Erickson, *The Road to Stalingrad* and *The Road to Berlin*.[15] Erickson, a professor at Edinburgh University, is a phenomenon. Like Richard Cobb for France, or Denis Mack Smith for Italy, he has succeeded in making himself into an expert on the history of a foreign country who commands both greater respect and greater consensus by his treatment of contentious issues in its past than one of its own nationals. Erickson learned Russian as a military intelligence officer after the Second World War — he insists, with pride, that the highest rank he held was sergeant in the field security police in occupied Austria — and became, through personal charm and evident integrity, the intimate of the highest-ranking members of the Soviet military hierarchy during the later Cold War years.

The war against Russia was undertaken by Hitler for many reasons — some ideological, some strategic — but economic factors may be judged to have predominated. Hitler feared the industrial might of the Soviet Union and coveted its agricultural and natural resources. Paradoxically, Operation Barbarossa deprived him of much that he wanted through both its destructiveness and the success of the Soviet government in evacuating beyond the Urals a high proportion of the country's engineering industry. What was left had to be brought back into production if Germany were to enjoy the anticipated benefits of the invasion undertaken to acquire them. A study which remains of abiding interest is Alexander Dallin's *German Rule in Russia*.[16] It reveals a record of managerial success — and failure — of direct relevance to our own times. Faced with a ruined industrial infrastructure that they badly needed to bring back into production, the Germans deployed a large number of managers, from such enterprises as Krupp and I.G.

Farben, to the occupied zone. They achieved some remarkable successes, largely through the application of incentives and market techniques of the sort the post-Soviet government is now trying to introduce to Russian industry worn down by fifty subsequent years of state planning. Collective agriculture, on the other hand, defeated the German effort to turn the clock back. There was no concerted attempt to reprivatize; German agronomists simply made the best local deals with farm managers that they could, leaving collectivized agriculture to return to Soviet control in 1944–45, with the lamentable consequences the post-Soviet government has inherited.

The devastation caused by the Germans and the disruption resulting from the emergency evacuation of industry to the east threw the Soviet government into a highly unwelcome dependence on its Western allies for aid of almost every sort, including raw materials as well as war equipment. Ironically its own oil industry, perhaps the principal prize Hitler sought to win through Operation Barbarossa but failed to capture, proved unable to deliver certain qualities of petroleum and lubricants; the shortfall was made up by American lend-lease. So were deficiencies in railway track, locomotives, and rolling stock, and, above all, in heavy road transport. U.S. supplies of 300,000 Dodge 6 x 6 trucks provided the mobility for the Red Army's advance to Berlin. There is an enormous literature in Western aid to Russia, but I have always found most of what I needed to know in a slim but incisive study, *Comrades in Arms* by Joan Beaumont.[17]

Economic shortcomings lay at the root of both Hitler's war aims and his strategic failures. A key text, of much wider interest than its title suggests, is Alan Milward's history of the German war economy.[18] One of a number of studies of economics at war, a subject he has made his own, Milward's book reveals how the German decision to fight for quick results off a narrow industrial infrastructure drew Hitler, once victory eluded him in 1940–41, to a series of short-term strategic decisions, each creating for him more difficulties than it solved. Thus, having failed to bomb Britain into surrender in the autumn of 1940 for want of a strategic air force — an air force deliberately not built because of the belief that quick victory would make one unnecessary — he was driven to secure his European conquests by turning on Russia; his failure to beat Russia in 1941, partly as a result of underinvesting in his tank fleet, forced him to strike for Russia's distant industrial heart in 1942, a target too remote for his insufficiently mobile army to reach; and so on.

There are many specialized studies of the way Hitler's strategy unfolded and of his command methods. Indispensable, I find, is the collection of his War Directives (*Führerweisungen*), seventy-four in number, edited and introduced by Hugh Trevor-Roper.[19] Nothing like them exists for either the American or the British side, where large decisions were collectively taken in cabinet or at an international conference. Through the Führer's Directive series we can follow, from the start,

Führerprinzip in action; later, the Directives reveal his increasingly ad hoc response to emergent crisis. More detail is supplied by the war diary of the Wehrmacht high command (OKW), in which the decisions of his twice-daily conferences are recorded, together with, at regular intervals, exact orders of battle for the different theatres of operations.[20] Largely compiled by a professional historian, Dr. Percy Schramm, they have not yet been translated into English, and are of great bulk, but yield vital information to any historian who seeks to establish a sequence of events for any of the campaigns in which the German armed forces were engaged. An intimate and human view of the context which produced the war diary is supplied by the deputy chief of operations officer at OKW, Walter Warlimont, in *Inside Hitler's Headquarters*.[21] OKW, a tiny inner staff, moved with Hitler as he shifted his location throughout the war, from Berlin to Berchtesgaden to Russia to France and back again. It remained for two long periods, however, at Vinnitsa in Ukraine and, after the Kursk defeat, at Rastenburg in East Prussia, scene of the bomb plot of July 20, 1944. Warlimont eerily recreates the atmosphere of isolation and unreality which enclosed Hitler's military household throughout the central years of his struggle to defy the world.

No similar studies are available to us of the inner workings of the Japanese high command. Indeed, Emperor loyalty and the alternative tradition of Japanese historiography, marked by a reluctance to ascribe decision to individuals, makes the appearance of any such study by a member of the war generation improbable. The best of introductions to the mentality which awoke the Japanese imperial instinct in the twentieth century are two books by an English historian, Richard Storrey, who had taught in Japan before the war and served in it as a Japanese-language intelligence officer. *A History of Modern Japan* depicts with lucidity the processes of modernization and the growth of the inferiority complex which made Japan a dangerous power in two senses; *The Double Patriots* unveils the character of the super-nationalism which carried Japan into war with China, and then with the Western powers.[22]

For a single-volume treatment of Japan's war itself, I depend upon Ronald Spector, formerly head of U.S. Naval History, who knows the subject intimately and writes with style and precision. *Eagle Against the Sun* has not yet been bettered as a compact, comprehensive history of that enormous war, which touched the Aleutian islands at its northernmost extent, northern Australia in the opposite direction, Madagascar to the west, and, if the Japanese balloon bombing of the American west coast is admitted as an act of war, California in the east.[23] Japan waged war by land as well as sea. The Pacific campaign was essentially, however, a maritime one, and its operational history has found a penetrating analyst in my former Sandhurst colleague, H.P. (Ned) Willmott. Only two volumes of what promises to be a four-volume work have so far appeared; their quality is sufficient to ensure that, when complete, the Willmott history of the Pacific naval war will be the standard work for the foreseeable future.[24]

These, then, are a selection of the books in which I have most come to depend for the story of the war as a whole and of the experience of the major combatants who took part in it. I have read much else — on Italy's war, Yugoslavia's, Poland's, and the experience of dozens of smaller countries over which the juggernaut rolled. Many are important; none is essential. What until recently has always been lacking, in my estimation, is some complete and convincing study of how the world came to be drawn into the catastrophe that the Second World War is now recognized to have been. A.J.P. Taylor's notorious study of the origins, represented by him as a series of short-term opportunity seekings, has now, having provoked the controversy its gadfly author desired, been largely discounted. More recently, my friend Donald Watt, after a lifetime of labour spent in the diplomatic archives, has produced a history which seems likely to remain unchallenged in his and my lifetime. *How War Came* is a history of the last year of peace, from the Munich crisis to the invasion of Poland, told, country by country, in penetrating detail and with serene intellectual certainty.[25] "Hitler," he writes in his conclusions, "willed, wanted, craved war and the desolation brought by war. He did not want the war he got." No one wanted the war he got, but it was certainly the war Hitler gave them.

CHAPTER THREE

BIOGRAPHIES

THE SECOND WORLD WAR WAS a conflict of personalities as well as peoples, to an extent that the First World War had not been. Great wars commonly call forth great leaders. America's Revolutionary and Civil wars produced Washington and Lincoln; the Thirty Years War, Gustavus and Wallenstein; Britain's long war of 1793–1815 against France, the younger Pitt, Nelson, and Wellington. It is unusual, at least in modern times, however, for a great war to be both provoked and directed throughout its course by a single man. Bismarck, who engineered the wars of German unification, did not command in the field, any more than Mazzini did during Italian unification.

It was because Napolean both chose to fight the war of the Third Coalition and oversaw all its major campaigns, often in person, that he for so long seemed a unique figure. Not until the coming of Hitler was Europe, and then the world, confronted with a warlord of similar political and strategic energy and ruthlessness.

Nothing explains how three of the powers Hitler chose to oppose — Britain, the Soviet Union, and the United States — succeeded in finding leaders who matched him in force of character. Churchill, Stalin, Roosevelt — though the Englishman and American must not be equated at the moral level with the Russian — resembled one another in fortitude. The First World War was, in some sense, a leaderless war. Clemenceau and Lloyd George found the determination to avoid defeat, Wilson the moral force to lead his nation into unsought hostilities; but it was a popular readiness to bear suffering, common to the people of Europe, which sustained their war effort to the point where American intervention, rather than the force of will exerted from the top, tipped the balance.

In the Second World War, exactly the opposite analysis holds true. Among Hitler's enemies, it was the will of the leaders which inspired, reinforced in Russia by Stalin's use of terror and repression. In Germany, it was Hitler who led his people to war, held them to bear its horrors, and directed every step of national strategy, and who relaxed his grip on power only when his own hand brought his life to an end in the war's last week.

The role of leadership in the Second World War invests biography with particular importance. There is a wealth of biographical, and autobiographical, material. Churchill and de Gaulle, indeed, both completed accounts of their war experience which succeed as both history and memoir.[1] The most valuable of books in this category, however, in my view, is one that has been called "the autobiography Hitler did not write" — David Irving's *Hitler's War*.[2] Irving is a controversial figure, an Englishman who has identified with the German war experience to a remarkable degree, who has offered a cash reward to anyone producing written evidence of Hitler's authorization of the "Final Solution," and who currently champions extreme right-wing politics in Europe. Nevertheless, he is a historian of formidable powers, having worked in all the major German archives, discovered important deposits of papers himself, and interviewed many of the survivors or their families and intimates.

Hitler's War is unique in that it recounts the war exclusively from the German side, and through the day-by-day thinkings and doings of Adolf Hitler. For Irving, Hitler is not a monster but the rational war leader of a great power, seeking to guide it to victory over other powers whose policies are as self-interested as Germany's. He is, nonetheless, a lonelier figure than Churchill or Roosevelt, and bears psychological burdens they did not. At least twice, during the Dunkirk campaign of 1940 and after the failure of the Stalingrad offensive in 1942–43, he experienced something akin to a nervous breakdown, short-lived in 1940 but prolonged in 1943. His loss of self-confidence after Stalingrad devolved power onto his subordinates, notably Zeitzler, his army chief of staff, and thereby drew Germany into the unwise Kursk offensive, which lost the Wehrmacht its tank reserve and so consigned it thereafter to fighting on the defensive. The picture Irving presents of Hitler is of a struggler amid great events, brilliantly successful at first, progressively borne down by circumstance as the odds lengthen against him, but resilient to the very end. If he accuses him of a single mistake, it is that of declaring war against the United States in the week of Pearl Harbor, a step nothing in the Tripartite Pact obliged him to do and against which Ribbentrop, his foreign minister, argued in vain.

Yet, Irving's Hitler is throughout a man who knows better what is good for Germany than do any of his helpmates or subordinates, who has recurrent flashes of military genius, who sacrifices his physical health to his cause, who eschews any personal friendship except that with an idealized German people itself. Among his cooperators, only Goebbels, his minister of propaganda, approaches him in vision and competence. The rest, even Himmler, self-proclaimed truest of the true, ultimately think of themselves. It is they who are responsible for the crassest errors — the policy of genocide foremost — and who betray both their leader and their country.

No historian of the Second World War can afford to ignore Irving. His depiction of Hitler, by its relation of

the war's development to the decisions and responses of
Führer headquarters, is a key corrective to the Anglo-
Saxon version, which relates the war's history solely in
terms of Churchillian defiance and the growth of the
Grand Alliance. Nevertheless, it is a flawed vision, for it
is untouched by moral judgment. For Irving, the Second
World War was a war like other wars — a naked struggle for national self-interest — and Hitler, one war leader
among others. Yet, the Second World War must engage
our moral sense. Its destructiveness, its disruption of
legal and social order, were on a scale so disordinate that
it cannot be viewed as a war among other wars; its opposition of ideologies, democratic versus totalitarian, none
the less stark because democracy perforce allied itself
with one form of totalitarianism in the struggle against
another, invariably invests the war with moral content;
above all, Hitler's institution of genocide demands a
moral commitment.

The moral dimension missing in Irving is found in the
second indispensable biography of war leadership,
Martin Gilbert's *Churchill*. Because of the length of
Churchill's life, Gilbert's work begins long before the
twentieth century, but the two volumes which cover the
war years, *Finest Hour* and *Road to Victory*, are rightly
the culmination to which the whole magisterial story is
directed.[3] In them, the chronological method the author
favours is supremely justified, for Churchill reacted to the
day-by-day unfolding of the war less by intellect, great
though his intellect was, than by force of character.

Churchill's moral character determined all he did. What Hitler was moved by, if by anything more than hatred, rancour, and the passion for revenge, remains mysterious; however, Churchill was moved by a passion for liberty and moral grandeur, above all the moral grandeur which his own country, first, and then the alliance of the English-speaking democracies, epitomized. His moral sense and almost mystical patriotism shine forth from every passage of Gilbert's books, illuminating every great decision he took. First, there was his burning belief in the greatness of France and his effort to keep it in the war at all costs, even to the point of proposing a political union of the two countries; then, there was the resolve to decline a negotiated peace with Germany, though invasion threatened and the Luftwaffe was bombing British cities; the decision to transfer the remnants of the British army to the Middle East followed, a decision taken so that the war against the Axis might be kept active, one of the bravest strategic judgments in the history of high command; from that ensued his decision to send much of the Middle Eastern army to Greece in 1941, committing it to a heroic failure that nevertheless proclaimed Britain's determination to defend its friends and oppose Nazi aggression at every point its armed forces could reach.

Churchill's principal strategic purpose throughout the dark years, however, had been to bring the United States into the war on Britain's side, an ambition founded on the knowledge that an American alliance alone would bring victory, but inspired by the belief that such an alliance was demanded by the ideals the two English-speaking peoples shared. Roosevelt was undoubtedly at one with Churchill in detesting the principles, or lack of principle, on which Nazism was founded. He was as great a libertarian as Churchill, and certainly a more committed populist. Nevertheless, Roosevelt, as an American patriot, conserved his own doubts about the exact nature of the threat offered by Hitler's Germany to the vital interests of his country. Cash and carry, lend-lease, "all means short of war" were testaments to the sense of common cause he felt with Churchill in the years before America's entry into the war. Without a direct challenge to American power, however, he could not bring that entry about. It was supplied, of course, by Pearl Harbor. There have been several studies of Roosevelt as war leader. By far the most convincing is the second volume of James McGregor Burns's full biography.[4] His main point is that, unlike Churchill, Roosevelt did not pride himself on the possession of particular strategic talent. He saw his role as that of sustaining the morale of the American people, sustaining the alliance, and ensuring that the results achieved by the war should benefit not only his own country but mankind itself.

Because Roosevelt did not involve himself in the day-to-day running of the war at the level of detailed decision-making practised by Churchill, an essential companion to the study of his war years is the remarkable biography of his chief of staff, General George C. Marshall, written by Forrest Pogue.[5] Marshall's role in

American government in the years 1940–45 was commanding. It was he who selected the army's future leaders, largely through his assessment of their performance in the Louisiana manoeuvres the year before war broke out; his choices were uncannily prescient. It was he who brought the unknown Eisenhower to Washington in the week of Pearl Harbor, placed him in the War Plans Division, rapidly promoted him as the scope of his strategic gifts were revealed, and sent him to London in the spring of 1942 to take up the responsibilities that would lead to his appointment as Supreme Allied Commander. Marshall was also ruthless in his refusals to appoint or promote. Old friendships counted for nothing once the war began; he selected exclusively on the basis of proven efficiency or evident promise. The same objectivity extended to his dealings with the president. Wary of Roosevelt's notorious capacity for talk and for getting his own way by charm, he made a resolution, to which he stuck, never to laugh at any of the president's jokes, or even to smile in his presence. He thus ensured that all the time they spent together was dedicated to the business in hand. It was time well spent. Marshall was a magnificent military manager, and the successful mobilization and higher direction of the American army and army air forces owed almost everything to him.

A study of Stalin as war leader from close hand is lacking. His immediate subordinates either did not publish memoirs or, if they did, wrote typically unrevealing Soviet officialese. We know, nevertheless, a good deal about Stalin's command methods from Erickson, who discloses the acute psychological crisis he suffered in the weeks after Operation Barbarossa and emphasizes his dependency on Zhukov, the most dynamic of his generals.[6] Recently, Alan Bullock, the biographer of Hitler, has come forward with a volume of parallel lives, Hitler's and Stalin's, and thereby supplied a satisfactory account of the Russian dictator at war.[7]

An exception to the dreary obfuscation of Soviet war memoirs can be found in V.I. Chuikov's account of the Stalingrad battle, *The Beginning of the Road*.[8] Chuikov commanded the Sixty-Second Army, which held the ruins of the city throughout the fighting. He writes with passion and frankness, and also with great compassion for the sufferings of the surviving citizens crouching in their cellars as the desperate struggle raged over their heads. He brilliantly portrays the reality of the crucial struggle for supremacy on the Eastern Front, but his book would stand on its own merits even if it were not the only patently truthful account of Russia at war that we have from the Soviet side.

The absence of any illuminating study of the Japanese high command at war has already been noted. A useful interim biography is Alvin Cox's *Tojo*, which examines the role of the general who effectively became head of the Japanese government in the war years.[9]

There is a wealth of biography of military leaders below the level of supreme command. Three particularly useful volumes are the series of collective studies of

Hitler's, Churchill's, and Stalin's generals written by teams of experts on the German, British, and Russian armies.[10] There are also excellent individual biographies and autobiographies. Memorable among biographies, outdated now in documentation but retaining its freshness and something of the sensation it caused when it appeared, is Desmond Young's *Rommel*.[11] Published in 1950, it was the first life of any German general of the Second World War to appear in English, if indeed not the first major military biography of the postwar years. It became an instant bestseller. Rommel had fascinated the British and won their grudging admiration. It was he who had run rings round the Desert Army in 1941–42, defying every effort to bring him to book; his tactical dexterity had invested Montgomery's victory over him at El Alamein with all the greater glory. It was he who had commanded in Normandy on D-Day and after, and whose death during the battle — as we now know, from suicide — had added greatly to the mystery surrounding the bomb plot against Hitler of July 20, 1944. Young unpicked the mystery and, in so doing, made Rommel all the more attractive. He became, through the book, a cult figure to the British, which he remains.

Two memoirs by other German generals have greatly influenced the historiography of the Second World War in the English-speaking world. The first is *Lost Victories* by Erich von Manstein, the supreme practitioner of mobile operations on any front; his exposition of what has come to be called the "operational" level of command, between tactics and strategy, has decisively influenced British and American military thinking in the postwar world.[12] *Panzer Leader*, by Heinz Guderian, was influential in a different way.[13] Guderian pioneered the use of the tank in the German army, and its use in large formations, and demonstrated to crushing effect how large tank formations could bring victory in the field, as his Panzer formation did in France in 1940. *Panzer Leader* — *Achtung! Panzer*, as it is more arrestingly titled in German — is a textbook of technical and military innovation, as well as an important record of how technical half-measures and industrial undercapacity led to Nazi Germany's defeat.

Another arm of the German armed forces underdeveloped for warfare against those of superior industrial powers was the Luftwaffe. Here, David Irving has again supplied a want by writing the most illuminating biography of its commander, Göring.[14] Göring was more than that. He was also, after the disappearance of Hess in May 1941, the Führer's heir apparent and, from before the war, had been director of the Four-Year Plan. His economic competence was sketchy, however, and that deficiency was reflected in his failure to lead the Luftwaffe into the era of full-blown strategic bombing. Its technical backwardness derived from an early decision to desist from the development of a long-range, load-carrying, multi-engined aircraft, a decision for which Göring must be accorded ultimate responsibility. Nevertheless, he remained popular with his pilots for much of the war and retained Hitler's confidence almost to the end. It was his premature attempt to assume the leadership, after Berlin had come under Russian siege, which caused his removal from the line of succession. At Nuremberg, he reasserted personal dominance over the other Nazi war criminals, impressed even the Allied prosecutors by his sangfroid, and in the end cheated the hangman by finding a means to commit suicide.

Dönitz, not Göring, was the subordinate whom Hitler ultimately chose to take on the leadership of the dying Reich. Like Göring, he had been a successful warrior in the Great War; unlike Göring, he led his army, the U-boat fleet, to great successes in the Second World War. Peter Padfield, his biographer, has shown that those successes were the fruit of careful forethought. In the era of disarmament imposed by the Versailles Treaty, when U-boats were forbidden to Germany, he worked out the tactics of a successful submarine offensive with surface torpedo craft, and they were applied almost unchanged during the Battle of the Atlantic after the U-boat fleet had been rebuilt.[15] Allied victory over the U-boats in 1943 was a near-run thing; had it not come, Britain would have starved, and the war might have been protracted for several years. Dönitz's powers of command and undeviating loyalty so impressed Hitler that his decision to nominate him as second and last Führer comes to seem, in retrospect, less of the surprise than it did at the time.

Everything about Hitler's court retains, nevertheless, the aura of unreality. It is conveyed arrestingly in the memoirs of his personal architect, Albert Speer, who rose to be director of the German industrial war effort.[16] Speer is a Faustian figure, a man of intellect and sophistication who failed to resist the seduction of power, even the overtly brutal power the Nazi system embodied, and who committed himself unreservedly to the Nazi state but retained sufficient detachment to recoil eventually from its nihilism and, in the end, to repent of his wrongdoing. *Inside the Third Reich* grips the attention of the reader from the outset by its portrayal of the excitement felt by the insiders who shared Hitler's rise to mastery over the Germans; it goes on to recount the means by which a war economy was managed in detail not available elsewhere; and it ends with a unique description of the disintegration of the Reich as Hitler's confederates sought to save their skins. Trevor-Roper's *Last Days of Hitler* continues to provide the best outsider's portrayal of the fall of the Nazi dictatorship; Speer's memoirs are an indispensable inside accompaniment to it.[17]

Biographies of the secondary figures in the anti-Hitler alliance must, of necessity, be of lesser interest or importance, since there the legitimacy of prevailing power subordinated the actions of generals and admirals to legal and national authority. Nevertheless, there is much to be learnt from such major works as Nigel Hamilton's *Montgomery*.[18] Monty, greatly disliked by many of his contemporaries though he was, is unarguably one of the war's great generals. The campaign in the desert was on a miniature scale compared with that on the Eastern

Front; had it, however, ended in a German victory, the strategic consequences, which included potentially a German advance to the oilfields of the Middle East, would have been grave; moreover, its successful conclusion transformed the morale of the British people, whose endurance in the front line of the alliance was of crucial significance to its fortunes. Montgomery, chosen by Churchill to lead the re-equipped and reinforced Eighth Army in a decisive test of arms against the apparently irrepressible Rommel, was a man of supreme self-confidence and high military skills. The victory of El Alamein was the outcome of his meticulous planning and unshakeable determination. A revisionist work which caused a sensation on its appearance, Correlli Barnett's *The Desert Generals*, attempted to belittle his achievement.[19] As time passes, however, that achievement comes to appear more remarkable than ever.

A counterpoint to Montgomery was his superior, Alexander, and a counterpoint to Hamilton's three-decker is Nigel Nicolson's slim, elegant, incisive biography, *Alex*.[20] Alex was everything Monty was not — an aristocrat, a charmer, something of an aesthete. He was not a great general, but he was the sort of soldier the British army liked and admired, as his American and other allies did also. His diplomacy towards the non-British contingents of the Allied confederation in the Mediterranean theatre contributed greatly to its success; his personal elegance and panache, to his own soldiers' confidence and self-regard.

The ethos of the American army is entirely different from that of the British, a bureaucratic and national institution rather than a coterie of regimental clubs. It is dominated by West Point, the forcing house of its leaders. Eisenhower was the quintessential West Pointer, a poor boy for whom his academy scholarship brought the gift of education and the promise of a career. He fulfilled it to the utmost. Stephen Ambrose, his biographer, conveys with acute sensitivity his family background in Abilene, Kansas; his painstaking rise to respectable rank in the tiny, pre-war army; and then his meteoric rise to supreme command.[21] British contemporaries of Eisenhower tended to depreciate his military skills; American critics, when he succeeded to the presidency, his political competence. I adhere to the view that he was a great man, both as soldier and as politician, and Ambrose's devoted but scholarly account of his life bears that opinion out.

Wars are won by good leaders but fought by their brave and often anonymous underlings. The Second World War has yielded a plethora of personal memoirs of the war experience at the small-unit and individual level. High on my list of outstanding war autobiographies stands E.B. Sledge's recollections of his time as a Marine in the Pacific War, *With the Old Breed*.[22] There was a particular horror to the Marine Corps' island fighting. At one moment, its soldiers were embarked passengers aboard ship, cramped and roughly fed but safely accommodated. At the next, they found themselves thrown into a maelstrom of fire against a deadly enemy in hand-to-hand combat. Sledge, now a retired professor of biology, has become a hero to his corps for his success in conveying, modestly but with gripping realism, the particular terror of Pacific amphibious warfare.

In a different theatre and an incomparably different style of warfare, Milovan Djilas also experienced the terror of sudden danger and hand-to-hand combat. One of the closest confederates of Tito in the partisan campaign to create "liberated areas" in Axis-occupied Yugoslavia, he followed his leader from mountain to mountain with the pursuing Germans on his heels, often escaping from their encircling clutches by minutes, yet never considering surrender, never relenting in the partisan mission to bring armed revolution to his country. *Wartime* is a book that might have been written in any country with a guerrilla tradition that underwent Nazi occupation.[23] It will be remembered as the key text of the Yugoslav war, and one of the most brilliant literary achievements of the Second World War itself.

Entirely different in tone — ironic instead of passionate — but equally literary in quality is a recently published British memoir of the war in Burma. George MacDonald Fraser has achieved fame as the creator of the character Flashman and now enjoys the ease of a bestselling author. As a teenager, he was conscripted into his local infantry unit, the 9th Battalion the Border Regiment, sent from Cumbria to the jungles of Southeast Asia, and cast head first into the hardship and occasional terror of close combat with the Japanese. Late, though it is, to appear as a personal memoir of the conflict, it has immediately been recognized as a classic both of Second World War writing and of the genre of military autobiography.[24]

A third memoir of the action, also late to appear, which seems destined to become a classic, is Alvin Kernan's *Crossing the Line*.[25] Kernan was a poor Wyoming boy, a child of the Depression, who enlisted as an ordinary seaman to escape a life without prospects in a rural backwater. Chance placed him aboard an aircraft-carrier in the Pacific before Pearl Harbor, and there consigned him to fly as an enlisted aircrewman in fighters and strike aircraft during the great air–sea battles of the war, from Midway to Okinawa. He survived the sinking of his first carrier, a ditching off another, and a series of aerial combats, for one of which he was awarded the Navy Cross. *Crossing the Line* is an extraordinary book, most of all for the sense it conveys of the isolation of the individual in an enormous, impersonal organization into which nevertheless, danger might at any instant intrude with an acutely personal immediacy.

From the enemy side, a book that has impressed me is the autobiography of a young German officer, Alexander Stahlberg, who served as aide-de-camp to the great Panzer general, von Manstein.[26] Stahlberg, like many upper-class young German officers, was aware of the growing hostility to Hitler that possessed the old officer corps once the tide of defeat set in after Stalingrad.

Though not a party to the Bomb Plot, he conveys the atmosphere in which it was planned with an insider's touch. The most interesting part of his book, however, is his description of his service before the war, a young conscript who became a reserve officer, in an army preparing to avenge the humiliation of 1918.

Finally, no English-speaking students of the war can afford to ignore two autobiographical novels. The first is James Jones's *The Thin Red Line*, an account, by an author who began life as an enlisted man, of the American pre-war army and of its involvement in the island battles of the Pacific.[27] Though it competes with the far better-known *The Naked and the Dead*, which launched Norman Mailer on his illustrious literary career, it is far superior to it. Second is Evelyn Waugh's trilogy — *Men at Arms, Officers and Gentlemen*, and *Unconditional Surrender* — in which a great novelist, perhaps Britain's greatest novelist of this century, renders in fictional form the national experience of defiance, survival, victory, and — for Waugh — disillusionment.[28] It is an essential companion to Winston Churchill's triumphalist history of their country's passage through the Second World War.

CHAPTER FOUR

CAMPAIGNS

WAR, ULTIMATELY, IS ABOUT FIGHTING, and this is as true of the Second World War as of any other. Despite the underlying importance of industrial capacity and relative technical superiority, of raw material supply, of strategic and tactical logistics, of labour skills and availability — all greater in the Second World War than in any before — success or failure on the battlefield determined the outcomes of all episodes for which those factors made preparation. Midway, the turning-point battle of the Pacific War, was a contest between American and Japanese maritime technology, expressed in numbers and quality of carriers and carrier aircraft deployed. In the

event, though the Japanese enjoyed superiority in numbers, and perhaps in quality, of shipborne aircraft, defec-
tive decision-making by the Japanese commander on the
spot, Admiral Nagumo, negated those advantages.
Midway was won by quicker and better American judgments, taken under pressure, and by a strong element of
luck, that stochastic ingredient of war-making which
material superiorities can never cancel out.

Campaign studies are well represented in the historiography of the Second World War. Rich in drama and
variety, the war provided official historians with plentiful
opportunity to exercise their craft and attracted in its
aftermath hosts of professional historians to the subjects
it offered; in turn, their output was swelled by the work
of survivors anxious to set their own experiences on
record. With certain exceptions, noted below, there are
no campaigns or major battles of the war that have not
been recounted in detail; most of its minor and obscure
engagements have also found their historians.

The exceptions start at the beginning. There still is no
satisfactory account in English of the German–Polish War
of 1939, which precipitated the general outbreak. The
Polish army — almost completely unmechanized, almost
without air support, almost surrounded by the Germans
from the outset and, shortly, completely surrounded
when the Red Army joined the aggression — fought more
effectively than it has been given credit for. It sustained
resistance from September 1 until October 5, five weeks,
which compares highly favourably with the six and a half

weeks during which France, Britain, Belgium, and Holland kept up the fight in the west the following year. One or two personal accounts illuminate the nature of the struggle; but, for a general treatment, we still depend on Robert Kennedy's semi-official account written for the U.S. Army and on Nicholas Bethell's later and more impressionistic *The War Hitler Won*.[1]

Equally, we lack an accessible account of the next episode of the war in Europe, the Soviet attack on Finland in the winter of 1939 and the unexpected stalemate that followed. Thomas Rics's *Cold Will*, a recent English study, is the best substitute.[2] There is better material on Germany's 1940 northern campaign, against Denmark and Norway. Denmark, surprised, unprepared, collapsed on the first day of the invasion, April 9, 1940; the Norwegians, fighting as resolutely as the Finns in their equally difficult terrain, protracted the campaign until after the invasion of France and the Low Countries had begun. François Kersaudy tells the story inspiringly from the Norwegian point of view.[3]

Despite having failed to conclude his Scandinavian offensive, Hitler launched his long-postponed attack against his French and British enemies as soon as the fine weather of 1940 came. We have an enormous number of accounts of those "sixty days that shook the West" from many sides. I continue to find the most satisfactory, as well as the most readable, Alistair Horne's *To Lose a Battle*.[4] A scholarly analysis is provided by Brian Bond, supplemented by the extremely thorough official history by L.F. Ellis.[5] No student of the campaign should fail to read *Strange Defeat*; Marc Bloch, its author, was the leading French historian of his generation, caught up in the war as a reserve officer, who conveys the paralysis and disorganization afflicting the French counter-effort to brilliant psychological effect.[6]

Among the many accounts of the war's next decisive episode, the Battle of Britain, Telford Taylor's remains undated.[7] Taylor, an American lawyer who worked at Bletchley Park and later prosecuted at Nuremberg, was a man of many talents, which included high historical gifts. An essential view of the struggle from the German side is provided in Williamson Murray's *Luftwaffe*, though that book is of value for all the campaigns in which the German air force took part.[8] While the air battle which would decide whether or not Britain could continue as a combatant was raging, another front had opened. The Italians, whom Mussolini had brought into the war in June, immediately invaded British-protected Egypt, thus challenging Britain's historic strategic position in the Mediterranean. An analysis of what that position signified and how it influenced Churchill's higher direction of the war is set out in Michael Howard's monograph précising his volume of the strategic official history.[9] Unfortunately, its quality is not matched by any of the many official accounts of the desert campaigns themselves, wholly though they occupied the British army's energies from 1940 to 1943. The period remains a challenge to a historian looking for a subject. Two caveats, however, must be entered: Correlli Barnett's biographical study of the desert generals is also an excellent guide to the campaigns they fought, while Anthony Mockler has written, in *Haile Selassie's War*, a brilliant record of the almost forgotten Anglo-Italian struggle for Ethiopia and the Horn of Africa, triumphantly concluded while the issue of decision in the Western Desert still trembled in the balance.[10]

Churchill's decision to transfer much of what remained of the British army after the fall of France from home to Egypt was one of astounding — if eventually justified — boldness. Even more bold, but barely justifiable, and then only in political rather than military terms, was his subsequent decision to embark much of the Expeditionary Force to Greece in the spring of 1941, to bolster the resistance of Britain's friends in southeastern Europe to inclusion within Hitler's Tripartite Pact. The expedition was a disaster, of which no satisfactory account has been written. The dependent disaster which resulted from it, the loss of Crete to a German airborne assault, has by contrast stimulated several historians to fine achievement — including Anthony Beevor, Alan Clarke, and I. Stewart.[11] Beevor's study is a model military monograph. It is complemented by a remarkable and highly literary personal memoir by a German officer who took part, Graf von der Heydte; his parachute regiment was later to experience the effects of airborne assault in reverse, when it defended the sector of Normandy into which the American parachute divisions dropped on D-Day.[12]

Britain's expulsion from southeast Europe was not to end its involvement with the region. The German invasion of Yugoslavia in April 1941, and that country's subsequent partition between its neighbours, including not only Italy but Hungary, Bulgaria, the Greater Reich, and Italian-occupied Albania, provoked the most effective guerrilla resistance that the Axis was to encounter anywhere outside Russia during the war. British involvement with the partisans, monarchist and communist alike, resulted in the production of some of the most graphic personal memoirs of the period, many passionate and polemic in tone. If none quite approached T.E. Lawrence's *Seven Pillars of Wisdom* in quality, it was not for want of trying. Outstanding are Fitzroy Maclean's *Disputed Barricades* and William Deakin's *The Embattled Mountain*, a recent American contribution, *Beacons in the Night*, by Franklin Lindsay, an officer of the O.S.S. operating through the facilities provided by the Special Operations Executive (SOE), is also arresting.[13]

Yugoslavia, despite the passions the fighting there provoked, was a secondary theatre of war. Its character epitomized, however, that of the far greater struggle in the east, which Hitler unleashed as soon as his Balkan conquests were completed. An essential guide to the transition between his western and Mediterranean and his Russian strategic commitment is Martin Van Crefeld's *Hitler's Strategy*, an early work by one of the world's foremost military historians.[14] The eastern war itself has been less well served by historical profession.

There are some 15,000 works in Russian, but almost all are marred by Soviet orthodoxies, and few, for that reason, have been translated. Alan Clark's *Barbarossa*, though dated and in some places slight, retains the qualities and freshness and broad sweep that won it excellent reviews when it appeared.[15] We still lack first-class treatments of the great encirclement battles of 1941, at Smolensk and Kiev, and of the defeat outside Moscow, the siege of Leningrad which resulted from the advance along the Baltic coast and caused the death by starvation of a million people over the next two years is, however, starkly recounted by L. Goure.[16] Stalingrad, the central event of the following year's campaign, after the Wehrmacht resumed the offensive, has been extensively written about, by contrast. Chuikov's remarkable memoir from the Russian side has already been noted; an excellent treatment by a Russian-language scholar, Geoffrey Jukes, is *Hitler's Stalingrad Decisions*.[17] Jukes is also the author of a useful account of Operation Citadel, the post-Stalingrad armoured battle of 1943, in which Hitler, his confidence temporarily shaken by the magnitude of the defeat on the Volga, deferred to his generals' opinion that the initiative should be resumed, and a decisive effort was made to break the Russian Front south of Moscow.[18] The outcome was even more disastrous than that of Stalingrad. In a fierce assault on a position defended by mines, artillery, anti-tank guns, and armour in very great depth, the German tank fleet suffered losses from which it never recovered. Hitler, unable to make good the devastation from current production, which had been decisively overtaken by Russian tank output, was thereafter forced to fight on the defensive, responding to Soviet initiatives rather than instituting offensives of his own.

During the winter of 1943–44 and the spring of 1944 the Red Army ground relentlessly westward, recapturing most of the ground lost to the Barbarossa blitzkrieg in 1941. By midsummer, its main force was positioned in Belorussia, opposite Army Group Centre. On June 22, it opened an offensive on a front of two hundred miles and destroyed the forces that stood in its path; the operation, code-named "Bagration" by the Russians, is known to Germans simply as "the destruction of Army Group Centre." There is an excellent, modern German account by Gerd Niepold, which has recently become available in English.[19] An immediate outcome of the Red Army's subsequent dash through Belorussia and eastern Poland to the banks of the Vistula was the decision taken by the commanders of the Polish Home Army to seize Warsaw from the German occupiers, in the hope of restoring a legitimate, non-communist government in the interval between the expected German withdrawal and the Red Army's arrival. It was a justifiable calculation but took no account of Stalin's readiness to let the Germans settle the postwar future of Poland in his favour. While the advance guard of the Red Army halted in the suburb of Praha, within sight of the old city of Warsaw, a picked force of German internal security troops ground down

Polish resistance until the survivors were forced to surrender; so fierce was it, however, that the Germans eventually agreed to treat combatants as prisoners of war in
order to bring the battle to an end. An excellent account
in English is *Nothing But Honour* by J.K. Zawodny, a
Polish author.[20]

Despite Bagration and the contemporaneous loss of
the Wehrmacht's positions in the west, Germany staged a
remarkable, if shallowly based, military recovery in the
winter of 1944, allowing it, among other things, to
launch the December Ardennes offensive into Belgium. In
the east, though it had abandoned Greece and most of
Yugoslavia to the Red Army and the partisans in the
autumn, it succeeded in holding Czechoslovakia and, in
Hungary, even in staging a counter-offensive at Lake
Balaton in March 1945. On the direct approaches to the
Reich, it also put up sturdy resistance. The purpose of the
fight was, in part, to allow the evacuation westward of as
many of the German-speaking peoples of the eastern
lands, German by citizenship or by culture, as could be
got away. Some seventeen million fled altogether, in conditions as brutal as any experienced by the victims of
Nazi aggression during the years in which the Wehrmacht
triumphed. This extraordinary episode is meticulously
documented by Christopher Duffy.[21] The Red Army's
advance was, nevertheless, relentless. It culminated in one
of the war's greatest battles, the battle for Berlin of
April–May, 1945, unforgettably narrated by Cornelius
Ryan, a master compiler of history from personal

accounts, in *The Last Battle*.[22]

Long before the Red Army recovered the initiative on the Steppes, the Western allies had already begun to hack into the perimeter of Hitler's strategic sphere of influence in the Mediterranean. An early German setback was the extinction of its foothold in Vichy-controlled Levant. There, in 1941, the British had been forced to fight a short, fratricidal war — Free French fought Vichy French in Syria and Lebanon — as A.B. Gaunson describes.[23] In the autumn of 1942, hard on the heels of Montgomery's victory at El Alamein, the British and Americans together assaulted Vichy's other Mediterranean stronghold in Algeria, Tunisia, and Morocco. These Torch landings met little resistance in Algeria or Morocco; a local armistice was rapidly arranged, and the Vichy forces came over to the Allied side. In Tunisia, however, the halting place of Rommel's desert army after its long flight from the El Alamein battlefield, Hitler decided to make a stand and reinforce. The battle for Tunisia was to be a bitter one, and, at Kasserine, to involve the tyro American army in a humiliating local defeat. An excellent study of this troubled, though eventually successful, opening of the Alliance's western assault on the Reich is Barrie Pitt's *The Crucible War*.[24]

Victory in Africa did not automatically smooth the unrolling of Anglo-American strategy for the rest of 1943. Washington retained hopes at the beginning of the year of opening a direct assault on Western Europe before its end. London demurred; Churchill and his chief of staff saw difficulties — of training, of choice of landing-place, of material disparity — and made them into stumbling blocks. The outcome, not greatly welcomed by Roosevelt and Marshall, was the decision to defer the great invasion until 1944 and to employ the Anglo-American Mediterranean forces meanwhile in an assault, first on Sicily, then on Italy. Churchill hoped also to include the Balkans and the Aegean islands in the strategic purview.

Mussolini's Italy had never had great enthusiasm for the war into which he led it. The upper class was Anglophile, the lower strongly linked to the United States by ties of emigration. Mussolini's early initiatives, the invasions of Greece, Egypt, and British Somaliland, led to humiliations from which, in Greece and North Africa, he had to be rescued by German intervention. The war also drew Italy into the guerrilla campaigns in the Balkans, and so eventually into the administration of policies of genocide. That challenged the conscience of many of the army's officers, who refused to obey or found means of obstructing deportations and massacres. A key text to this episode, which epitomizes Italian attitudes to the war, is Jonathan Steinberg's study of the Italian army before and after the armistice in 1943.[25] The fighting in Sicily and Italy is best recounted in Bidwell and Graham's history; the part played by Italians after the armistice, both by regulars and partisans, by Richard Lamb.[26] Churchill did succeed, as a by-blow to this campaign, and against American advice, in committing British troops to the reconquest of the Aegean islands, whose Italian garrisons came over to the Allied side after September 1943; the disastrous results, which included a complete British defeat and the massacre of many Italians recaptured by their former German allies, is described by Jeffrey Holland, who took part.[27]

Churchill's hope had been that the invasion of Italy would so weaken German powers to resist inside Fortress Europe that a cross-Channel invasion would thereby be greatly facilitated, perhaps even rendered unnecessary. In practice, Hitler was able to defend Italy successfully with forces inferior to the Allied attackers, without drawing to any significant extent on the army garrisoning France. As a result, the invasion of Normandy in 1944 had to be launched with the greatest available sea, air, and land force. The enterprise has still not been better analysed than by Chester Wilmot. Valuable later accounts are supplied by Max Hastings, Carlo d'Este, and Alexander McKee; my own *Six Armies in Normandy* recounts the cause of the campaign from the points of view of the major combatants engaged.[28]

In the aftermath of the Normandy triumph, which carried the invading armies to the frontiers of the Reich a year ahead of schedule, some Allied leaders came to believe that the war might be finished by Christmas. One was Montgomery, who pressed Eisenhower as Supreme Commander into permitting the use of the Allied Airborne Army to lead a land–air assault across the Dutch rivers to the gateway of the German plains. The operation, Market Garden, was only a partial success;

the farthest landing, at Arnhem, was quickly contained by the Germans, and the British 1st Airborne Division largely destroyed in the process. The tragic battle has been much written about; new light is thrown on it by Robert Kershaw, a serving British parachute officer, who has worked extensively in the German archives.[29] Meanwhile, the Wehrmacht was reorganizing its broken troops on another river position, the mouth of the Scheldt. By holding it, the Germans were able to strangle the Allied logistic effort throughout the autumn and set back the final offensive against Germany by many months. Accounts of how the reorganization was achieved are fascinatingly supplied by Milton Shulman, who interviewed many of the German commanders involved immediately after the war.[30] Among the consequences of the failure at Arnhem and the delay on the Scheldt was Hitler's final western offensive, the Battle of the Ardennes, or "Bulge," as it became known to Americans. The set-back, though profoundly embarrassing to Eisenhower, was of no lasting strategic significance. German success in surprising and overwhelming many American formations in the front line nevertheless cast doubt on the quality of the U.S. army. Such doubts have subsequently been repudiated. Outnumbered American units fought with great courage and tenacity, as the accounts of John Eisenhower, the Supreme Commander's son, and others have now established.[31] The Ardennes was, in any case, the Wehrmacht's last gasp in the west; it put up a poor resistance to the Allied assault in the Rhine in the spring and swiftly collapsed during the fighting inside Germany that followed; the final stages of the Second World War in the west have not yet received a satisfactory historical treatment.

The German surrender was formalized on May 8, 1945. The war in the Pacific, Southeast Asia, and China still had four months to run. Its opening may be dated eight years earlier, when Japan broke out of the extraterritorial settlement in Shanghai in a campaign of naked aggression designed to incorporate the richest areas of the Chinese republic within its economic empire. A useful though necessarily incomplete account of the war that ensued is supplied by Richard Wilson.[32] Japan's aggression against China engaged the disapproval from the outside of the United States, which had established deep cultural and commercial links with the Chinese people during the second half of the nineteenth century. America had also, of course, been responsible for the opening of Japan to the outside world from 1854 onwards. Its diplomatic expertise in the Pacific region was considerable; in its effort to restrain the ultra-nationalism of army-dominated Japan after 1937, however, it fell into a series of miscalculations. Rightly identifying the country's economic weakness, it conceived a policy of bringing it to heel by the threat of cutting off its supply of essential raw materials, including oil and non-ferrous metals. The imperial government decided, though warned of the inevitability of defeat by Admiral Yamamoto, not to back down but to go on the offensive. The outcome was the surprise attack on the American Pacific Fleet in Pearl Harbor. There are no satisfactory accounts of the event, which remains clouded by allegations of concealed fore-knowledge, possessed by both Roosevelt and Churchill. Overlong and ill-organized though it is, Gordon Prang's *At Dawn We Slept* must suffice as the nearest thing to a definitive history.[33]

Yamamoto, Commander of the Japanese Combined Fleet, had warned that the best outcome Japan could hope for was the freedom to "run wild for six months or a year." His lower forecast was borne out almost to the week. On June 4, 1942, an inferior force of U.S. aircraft-carriers was enabled, by brilliant intelligence deception and decryption, to entrap the Combined Fleet into a long-distance duel which resulted in the sinking of two-thirds of its strength. There have been many books on the Battle of Midway; the most reliable and arresting remains Samuel Eliot Morison's volume in the official history.[34]

Meanwhile, however, Japan had occupied French Indo-China by subjecting the Vichy regime to demands for bases in the colony it lacked the means to resist, had invaded British Malaya and destroyed the fleet sent to protect it, and had also conquered the Dutch East Indies. An old but still interesting book on the key episode, the sinking of H.M.S. *Prince of Wales* and *Repulse*, is Richard Grenfell's.[35] We still await a good history in English of the Japanese blitzkrieg in the Dutch colonial possessions.

The Japanese plan of operations in Southeast Asia also embraced the conquest of Burma. In a continuation of their lightning advance through Malaya and to Netherlands East Indies, they succeeded in driving the British and Indian defenders out of the cities and the plains but could not expel them from the mountain frontier with India. There the British reorganized and instituted the beginnings of a counter-offensive which, after many false starts and set-backs, was eventually to culminate in a triumphant reconquest. Louis Allen's *Burma: The Longest War* is not only the best history but also one of the most comprehensive and many-faceted campaign studies of the war in any of its theatres. It should be read in conjunction with the record written by the commander of the British-Indian Fourteenth Army, William Slim, and with the autobiography of one of the officers who fought behind Japanese lines with the Chindits, John Masters.[37]

Even more bitter than the battles fought to reconquer Burma were the U.S. forces' attacks on the oceanic perimeter Japan had staked out after Pearl Harbor. These were set-piece amphibious attacks on fiercely defended islands by the U.S. Navy, Marines, and Army, to which vast sea battles were often the preliminaries. William Manchester's biography of the commander in the South Pacific is an essential introduction to the strategy of that zone; J.D. Potter's life of Nimitz covers the Central Pacific.[38] American strategy, drawing on the resources of their vastly superior air and sea mobility, was to drive corridors into the Japanese oceanic frontier, taking some key islands, while leaving others to "wither on the vine." In 1944, the drive from the south converged with that in the Central Pacific, culminating in the sea and ground battle for the Philippines. Falk's *Decision at Leyte* recounts the preliminary sea battle, in terms of ships, engaged the largest ever fought; Smith's *Triumph in the Philippines*, the land victory.[39] The ordeal of the final approach to the Japanese home islands remained to be endured. The essential stepping-stones were the islands of Okinawa and Iwo Jima, both to be the scenes of desperate and bloody engagements. The latter was to be the worst in terms of human suffering; the former has attracted better historical treatment, notably in Appelman's compendium.[40]

Even after the fall of the nearest islands, the Allies — for Britain had sent a fleet to join the great American Pacific Armada — expected that a final and enormously costly conventional invasion of Japan would have to be mounted. That was to be rendered unnecessary by the presidential decision to use the secretly developed nuclear weapon on Japanese centres of population against first Hiroshima, then Nagasaki. Useful accounts of this terrible episode and of the Japanese reaction to it are provided by H. Feis and J.F.C. Butow.[41] One school of historians continues to insist, however, that, even before Japan had been subjected to nuclear bombardment, it had accepted that capitulation was the only option, as a result of the Soviet blitzkrieg into Manchuria, of which David Glantz provides an admirable account.

The essence of many ·of these individual campaign studies is encapsulated in perhaps the most useful of all study guides to the Second World War, *The West Point Atlas of American Wars*, edited by Vincent J. Esposits.[43] Designed as an accompaniment to the history courses taught at the U.S. military academy, its brief texts and its beautiful maps, drawn by the academy draughtsman, Ed Krasnaborski, are the most satisfactory résumé of the Second World War's development and resolution anywhere. Finally, however, and perhaps immodestly, I might suggest that *The Times Atlas of the Second World War*, which covers economic, political, and social aspects of the conflict, can also be used with profit.[44]

CHAPTER FIVE

THE BRAINS AND SINEWS
OF WAR

WAR, THOUGH ULTIMATELY ABOUT FIGHTING, is also about planning where and when to fight, and disguising one's intentions from the enemy while seeking to penetrate his.

Commanders have always sought to deceive, and have put an equivalent effort into protecting themselves against surprise, chiefly through espionage and the interception of the enemy's communications. In no war before that of 1939–45, however, had intelligence been accorded a greater importance. The rapidity of operations, vastly accelerated by the internal-combustion engine and the aeroplane, and the greatly enhanced destructive effect, particularly on civilian targets, of modern weapons lent unprecedented urgency to the search for fresh ("real time") and accurate information. It lent equal weight to the need to hide the meaning and destination of signals, particularly since the scale and pace of the fighting necessitated ever greater dependence on the new medium of radio. Such factors are what allow us to talk about the Second World War as an "intelligence war."

The greatest secret of the Second World War was that, from as early as 1940, the Western allies were reading the German secure radio ciphers, and, from 1941 on, were reading them extensively and in "real time." The German armed forces had adopted in the 1930s a commercial cipher machine, the Enigma, as its instrument of encryption; capable of 200 million possible transpositions for any single letter entered on its typewriter keyboard, it was believed to produce unbreakable encipherments. Work by the Polish intelligence service before 1939 had shown the belief to be false and, during the Phoney War, the work done by the Polish mathematicians was donated to the British and French teams also struggling with Enigma. After the fall of France, the British anti-Enigma attack was concentrated at the Government Code and Cipher School at Bletchley Park, to which were recruited first-class mathematicians, linguists, and other possessors of appropriate talents from Oxford, Cambridge, and similar centres of learning. They began to make rapid progress, partly by direct attack on the logicalities of the encipherment, partly by recognizing and exploiting mistakes made by the German users of the machine in day-to-day transmissions, Luftwaffe users were the least careful, and it was a Luftwaffe "key" that was broken first; breaks into the army and naval keys followed; but, it should be noted, some keys were never broken. Keys were also lost, sometimes for long periods, when Germans made changes or complexified the machine or tightened up procedures. The naval key was lost, with grave effects on the conduct of the Battle of the Atlantic, during 1942–43; all the graver was the loss because the German equivalent of Bletchley, the B-dienst (Observation Service) was meanwhile reading British naval signals, which were still being disguised inside an obsolete book code.

At the height of the intelligence war, ten thousand people worked at Bletchley. All were sworn to secrecy — and the secret was kept until 1974, when, for reasons which have never been fully explained, a former Bletchley initiate, Group Captain F.W. Winterbotham, was allowed to publish an undocumented account of Bletchley's wartime work.[1] "Ultra" was the cover name given at Bletchley to the Enigma decrypts; Winterbotham's book opened the floodgates. After its appearance, the government could no longer, though it consistently tried, forbid "B.P." people from adding to the revelations. Indeed, it already had in preparation an official account of its own, to which Winterbotham's book may have been intended as a trailer. F.H. Hinsley, a Bletchley officer who had won there a glittering reputation as an interpreter of Ultra decrypts and who went on to fulfil his undergraduate promise by becoming a Cambridge professor of history, published in 1979 the first of what were to be four volumes on the influence of British intelligence on the conduct of strategy and operations.[2] When completed, the work, by far the most arresting of the whole official series, told an astonishing story. It revealed the existence of a worldwide network of "special intelligence," whose officers were supplied daily with Bletchley intercepts and empowered to distribute their contents, carefully disguised as to source, to a chosen élite; it also revealed how many — the vast majority — of commanders and government servants were ruthlessly excluded from the Ultra secret.

It also revealed how, in order to preserve the source of Ultra, the Germans were frequently allowed to achieve successes which could only have been negated at the risk of compromising the system; thus, for example, Ultra supplied accurate early warning of the intended German airborne invasion of Crete, but appropriate countermeasures were not taken, since to take them would have been to indicate to the attackers that the British defenders, weak and disorganized, had foreknowledge.

In a postscript to his great work, a compilation of memoirs by Bletchley inmates which he co-authored with Alan Stripp, Hinsley made comparatively modest claims for what Ultra achieved.[3] He denied that it "won the war," or even greatly altered its course. It did, he believed, however, shorten the war, in particular by averting disaster in the Battle of the Atlantic and by permitting the Allies to launch the invasion of Europe in 1944 "on tight margins," rather than in 1945, by which time Germany would have made operational revolutionary U-boats and improved pilotless weapons. Hinsley's conclusions are not to be argued with; as a master player of the game, he can make judgments not open to the rest of us. Nevertheless, perhaps he underplays the significance of the confidence that possession of the Ultra secret gave to the high command, American and British alike.

From September 1943, Bletchley ceased to be an exclusively British organization. Under an agreement to pool intelligence, akin to that regarding the pooling of nuclear research, American officers began to join the Ultra teams; one of them was Telford Taylor, already mentioned as a future historian of the Battle of Britain. What made the sharing of equal value was that the Americans had, in an effort equivalent to Bletchley's, succeeded in breaking the Japanese machine cipher, codenamed "Purple," and from it derived information which led, for example, to the identification of Midway as Japan's strategic objective in mid-1942 and, in 1943, to the interception and destruction of the aircraft in which Yamamoto, its leading admiral, was making a tour of inspection. The story of the making of the intelligence agreement is told by Bradley Smith in a recent book. The wider implications of the American penetration of Purple are analyzed by Ronald Lewin.[5]

It is the workings of Bletchley, however, which have

generated the larger and more arresting literature. A book of the greatest importance is Gordon Welchman's.[6] He was a mathematician who was the first to design methods of breaking into the Enigma system using its own rules rather than their breach. The book contains the best available explanation of how Enigma worked. An even more important mathematical mind was Alan Turing's; it was he who wrote the theoretical description of a non-mechanical computer before any had been built and oversaw the construction of the first model, the Colossus, which matched the Enigma machine at its own game. [7] Any consideration of the technical achievements of Bletchley must, however, take account of the work of the Polish pioneers, discussed by W. Kozaczuk.[8]

The story of Enigma is unusual in the historiography of intelligence in that it has prompted several enquiries into how it actually affected the conduct and results of operations. Ralph Bennett, an Oxford historian who worked at Bletchley, has achieved that most difficult of tasks, demonstrating the direct effect of intelligence-gathering on the outcome of campaigns. In *Ultra in the West*, for example, he shows how Hitler's final attempt to contain the American break-out from Normandy in August 1944, the Mortain counter-attack, was checked by the prepositioning of an American armoured division athwart the axis of the Panzer thrust before it could be launched; timing and location were decided by Ultra decrypts of German orders.[9] The achievement of Ultra in the Mediterranean was patchier. Before the German airborne invasion of Crete in May 1941, it had supplied a clear picture of enemy intentions; such was the weakness of the defence, however, that not even accurate pre-knowledge sufficed to defeat them. Again, during the early stages of the desert war, Ultra often exposed what Rommel proposed, but his skill on the battlefield outwitted even forewarned opponents. The arrival of Montgomery altered the balance. A doughty and cunning fighter, he was enabled by Ultra to position his troops correctly to thwart Rommel's final bid to advance on Alexandria, and then to exploit Axis weakness in his own triumphant counter-offensive at El Alamein. Ultra later confirmed the success of the Allied measures to deceive Hitler over the objectives of a cross-Mediterranean amphibious invasion and so open the way to an assault on Sicily.[10]

The greatest achievements of Ultra, however, were won at sea. Naval warfare is peculiarly sensitive to the disclosure of information about the position and destination of ships and fleets, their armament and mission, their speed and heading. Much of naval warfare, indeed, is directed towards achieving or avoiding encounter at sea, and captains and admirals have sometimes won stunning victory by intelligent interpretation of the smallest scraps of intelligence about the movements of the enemy. Ultra offered the possibility of acquiring, not scraps, but reams of intelligence about the movements of the U-boats, which were the deadliest menace to Britain's survival. For that reason, the German naval staff devised a particularly secure means of Enigma transmission within the submarine fleet and also devoted great effort to penetrating the British codes through which the convoys and their escorts were controlled. As a result, something which may be called a true "radio intelligence war" was fought out over the wastes of the North Atlantic in 1941–43, in which the balance swayed from side to side. In 1941, the Admiralty was reading Enigma regularly; during much of 1942, a blackout descended when the Germans altered the machine; it did not lift until March 1943. Worse, during much of this period, the crisis of the U-boat war, the German interception and decrypting service, the B-dienst, was breaking the Royal Navy's obsolete book code, to the great benefit of U-boat operations. Patrick Beesly has recounted the events of the struggle.[11] David Kahn, the historian of codes and ciphers, explains the technicalities in *Seizing the Enigma*, a gripping and tautly written narrative of captures of key equipment and papers at sea and of the use made of them at Bletchley Park.[12]

Signal intelligence — "Sigint" — is the best of all sources of day-to-day information in war. Human intelligence — "Humint" — may provide something superior, a guide to the enemy's long-term plans and way of thinking. It is the most difficult to acquire, since it depends upon the existence of agent or agents "in place." British intelligence was hampered by the "rolling up" of its network of agents in Europe at the outset of the war, as C. Andrew points out.[13] The United States had never succeeded in penetrating the secretive and alien society of Japan. Only the Soviet Union, through the ideological loyalties it was able to manipulate as centre point of the Communist International, enjoyed access to the inner councils of its enemies. The "Red Orchestra" was the most important of its networks inside Germany; the most highly placed of its spies was Richard Sorge, a German communist serving as a foreign correspondent in Tokyo, who, through his unofficial but intimate relationship with the German embassy there, supplied Stalin with timely warning of Japanese strategic intentions in the Far East.[14]

Deprived though the British were of direct human intelligence within Germany, they were able to influence German intelligence perceptions by their remarkable success in "turning" all German agents inserted into the United Kingdom during the war. Once under British control, they misinformed their German masters about much; crucially, during the pilotless weapons campaign of 1944–45, about the points of impact of V-1 and V-2 missiles, thus sparing London damage.[15] More controversial is the value of the effort the British, and, later, the Americans, invested in "special operations," the subversion of the Nazi empire from within. Churchill, a devotee of undercover warfare since his Boer War days, set up the Special Operations Executive (SOE) on July 16, 1940, with orders to "set Europe ablaze." Its mission was to raise guerrilla forces within the occupied countries, to supply them with arms, and to provide them with trained officers as advisers and leaders. [16] The mission met with varied fortunes. In France, where the SOE had to mediate between competing resistance organizations owing allegiance to different masters — the Communist Party, de Gaulle's Free France — it did little to impede German military operations, though extravagant claims have often been made to the contrary.[17] In Belgium, Holland, and Denmark, small countries crushed by the weight of occupation, it achieved nothing of substance. Poland, though its Home Army was to raise a heroic resistance in Warsaw in August 1944, was too distant for the SOE's apparatus to operate effectively.[18] Only in the Balkans, accessible from the SOE's Middle Eastern headquarters in Cairo, and heir to centuries of guerrilla resistance to Ottoman occupation, did its officers take the role Churchill had perhaps envisaged for it in 1940.[19] Their intervention in Yugoslavia, scene of a civil war as well as an insurrection, has been the cause of abiding controversy, which remains so heated that there can be no definitive account as yet. The most celebrated of accounts is William Deakin's memoir of his months with Tito;[20] a polemical version of the story from the Chetnik side is *The Rape of Serbia* by Michael Lees, a liaison officer with Mihailovic.[21] Towards the conclusion of the Yugoslav campaign, the SOE's American equivalent, the Office of Strategic Services (OSS), also took a part; a recent personal account of the highest quality is *Beacons in the Night* by Franklin Lindsay, a young and dashing OSS officer.[22]

No general survey or analysis of the impact of the

intelligence war on the war itself has yet been written. Conclusions are elusive. Intelligence is a subtle and fluid commodity; war is brutally material. Increasingly, in the age of industrialism, its principal and lasting effects have been achieved through attrition, the wearing-down of resistance by the destruction of lives, and industrial resources and their output of war material to the front. Attrition, the Materialschlacht, had underlain Allied victory in the First World War, unfairly in the view of the German General Staff, which took the not-unjustified view that its armies had fought the more skilful fight. In the period of rearmament before the Second World War, Germany made an affirmative decision not to be outclassed materially again; it had failed to match the Allies at the technical level particularly, and so embarked on a productive program of tank and high-performance aircraft development. The program paid off; in 1939–40, the German armoured and aerial fleets outmatched those of the enemy, certainly in quality and arguably in size. There was, nevertheless, a persisting defect in the German war economic policy. It was dedicated to quick victory, not to the long attritional haul; the policy has been characterized as one of "blitzkrieg economics." Against Britain, a weaker economy, Germany's industrial strategy worked. Once the Soviet Union, and then the United States, the world's leading industrial power, were drawn in, the structural weaknesses in the German war machine were displayed to fatal disadvantage. In the period 1940–45, for example, German industry turned out some 40,000 tanks and 100,000 aircraft; but, meanwhile, the Soviet Union produced 100,000 tanks and 137,000 aircraft, and the United States 86,000 tanks and more than 300,000 aircraft, 90,000 of the latter in 1944 alone.

From the beginning of 1942, therefore, Germany found itself caught again in a *Materialschlacht* in which the odds were stacked against it. Alan Milward, the leading economic historian of the Second World War, has exposed the nature of the German dilemma in *The German Economy at War*.[23] He has also described the efforts made by Germany to expand its economic base by subordinating the manufacturing and extractive industries of the occupied countries to its policies in a series of important monographs, including studies of the French and Norwegian war economies.[24] None of these efforts availed. The disparities were too great, as his masterly overview of the whole economic war scene, *Economy and Society, 1939–45*, reveals.[25]

The picture is thrown into starker contrast when viewed from the other side. The United States in 1940, when it began its rearmament, to equip both its own armed forces and those of Hitler's opponents, was working far below its capacity. The effects of the crash of 1929 and the subsequent depression persisted. In 1940, American industrial plant utilization averaged forty hours per week; by 1944, ninety hours. In 1940, 8.7 million Americans were unemployed; by 1944, all those had been drawn back into the work force, along with 10 million new workers. Gross national product, which stood at $88 billion in 1940, rose to $135 billion in 1944. Output of manufactured goods rose by 300 per cent, and of raw materials by 60 per cent; overall, the productive capacity of the economy increased by 50 per cent. All this was achieved, moreover, without serious damage to civilian consumption, which actually increased during the war years, despite the dedication of industrial capacity to military purposes, by 12 per cent. The war made the United States rich again; Studs Terkel, the American oral historian, recorded the testimony of a National Youth Administration worker who had gone off to war in 1941: "the war was a hell of a good time. Farmers in South Dakota that I administered relief to [during the Depression] and gave 'em bully beef and four dollars a week to feed their families, when I came home were worth a quarter of a million dollars, right? What was true there, was true all over America....World War Two? It's a war I would still go to."[26]

The economic effects elsewhere were almost universally the contrary. The war made winners and losers alike poor, in some cases destitute. The individual food ration in Germany in 1946 was actually lower in nutritional content than the minimum necessary to support life; Japan in 1945 was employing two million people to grub up pine roots, from which a crude petroleum substitute could be distilled. Once the tide of war set against the Axis partners, neither outcome could have been avoided. Their wartime economic policies, however, contributed to the calamity. Both had looked to external sources in occupied countries for the supply of agricultural produce and raw materials, while subordinating their own economies to the production of war materiel. When defeat deprived them of access to external supply, their industrial resources, which had been dedicated to war production, could not earn the foreign exchange necessary to support their populations. They became dependent on the charity of their conquerors. The record of this doleful decline is narrated in a variety of sources, of which Bisson's and Carr's are indispensable.[27] A wider view of the impact of Japan's economic imperialism is provided by F.C. Jones; co-prosperity, as Japan dubbed it, proved in practice to mean prosperity for Japan and economic subservience for its unwilling Asian partners.[28] Italy, theoretically Germany's partner but practically its dependant, suffered a similar economic dependency, with catastrophic effects on control of its own industry and manpower.[29]

The least equal effects of the war were borne by Britain, a strategic victor but a net economic loser. The world's leading creditor nation in 1939, its isolation after June 1940 required it to liquidate the majority of its foreign holdings in the period when it stood "alone," simply to buy essential raw materials and foodstuffs on the open market; not until the 1980s would it restore its foreign investments to the pre-war level. Britain, however, suffered more than financially. Great damage was done to the structure of its cities by Luftwaffe bombing, particularly in industrial and dock areas; industry was starved of investment in the war years; the dedication of national income to war production, in a fiscal regime that averted inflation, eroded private and public capital very steeply. Much war production was simply of a replacement nature; though British shipyards launched a thousand ships every year between 1940 and 1944, sinkings were higher, and Britain was supplied in 1941–43 only because foreign owners could be tempted into the charter market by elevated war rates.[30] Britain ended the war, in every sense, a poorer country than it had been at the outset.

A compensation of the costs of war-making in the industrial age is commonly held to be that derived from technological innovation under the pressure of military events. Discovery, substitution, rationalization — all are effects that war is held to stimulate. There is undoubtedly something to this argument. Britain, for example, which mobilized a higher proportion of its population than any other combatant, sustained, and even increased, output during the war, partly by depressing civilian demand by 21 per cent below 1939 levels, partly by conscripting women to replace men in almost every sector of employment, except for mining and the heaviest of heavy industry. On the other hand, the bureaucracy of control exerted over industry, labour use, consumption, and freedom of movement and residence was in itself labour-intensive. Employment went up; not all of it could be considered useful employment by market standards.

Moreover, investment in innovative technology was too war-specific to yield benefits of wide post-war applicability. British electronics made remarkable advances in radar and computing; so, too, did mechanical engineering, which produced high-quality aero engines, including jet engines. However, the demand for volume necessitated in most productive sectors a repetitive output of established designs, obviating ventures into new technology.

Britain found itself, moreover, increasingly forced to specialize in certain categories of war production, particularly of fighter and bomber aircraft, leaving the United States to make up deficiencies in shipping, tanks, and wheeled transport. In the United States, the war raised production in all sectors of industry and stimulated remarkable advances in the techniques of prefabrication and substitution, including artificial rubber and man-made fibres.[31] Britain, by contrast, became a less, not more, diverse industrial power, subordinating its manufacturing to that of the "Arsenal of Democracy" in the pursuit of common victory. In some sense, it followed the same path, willingly rather than compulsorily, that France and the other German-occupied countries of Europe took behind German industry during the war years. Germany's industrial policy towards the conquered nations was initially purely exploitative; they were to supply raw materials, food, and labour, while German factories produced military materiel. By 1943, however, the German war planners — Albert Speer, foremost — had seen that a more intelligent policy was to engage the industrialists of conquered Europe in partnership. It was a partnership that suited both parties, yielding higher outputs than would have been available to Germany by brutal exaction and actual profit to French, Belgian, and Dutch factory owners. The key figure in the arrangement was a French civil servant, Jean Bichelonne, who agreed with Speer in September 1943 on a system of planning and tariff reduction in which many see the origins of the postwar Iron and Steel Community, Common Market, and eventual European Union.[32] It is significant in this context that Norway, the first country in Europe to have resisted by popular vote accession to the European Union, was also the country on which Germany tried to impose the most extensive measures of economic integration during the Second World War.[33]

In one sector of war production, however, the integration of effort was of undoubted mutual benefit as well as of strategic value. That was in the nuclear weapons program, which, as early as the spring of 1940, Britain had accepted as viable. One of the emergency measures taken during the fall of France was to ensure the transportation to Britain of the French supply of heavy water essential to the building of a nuclear reactor. By July 1941, Britain had decided to embark on the building of a uranium-235 bomb, but in 1943, when it became clear that national resources would not suffice to bring the program to a successful conclusion swiftly enough to avert the possibility of Germany's doing so also, the government agreed with the United States to pool all knowledge, manpower, and materiel in a joint effort. Britain's initial contribution was eventually dwarfed by America's, but the impetus of the Manhattan project was owed to Britain's alarm that Hitler might acquire the atomic bomb first.[34]

As we know now, the dispersion of scientific effort within Nazi Germany so held back Hitler's atomic weapons program that, by 1945, it was still years away from developing a bomb. That discovery did not invalidate the urgency which underlay the Anglo-American program. In another sector of weapons research, eventually to be thought an essential element of nuclear strategy, Germany far outstripped the Allies. Pilotless weapons, which would become the means of delivery of the American nuclear warhead, were a German invention. By June 1944, Germany was bombarding Britain with cruise missiles; on September 8, the first ballistic rocket landed on London.[35] Its impact inaugurated the missile age. The outcome of a war in which Nazi Germany came to possess both pilotless and nuclear weapons is too dreadful to contemplate.

CHAPTER SIX

OCCUPATION AND RESISTANCE

THE SECOND WORLD WAR SUBJECTED almost the whole continent of Europe and the most productive regions of East Asia to foreign military occupation. The response of those varied greatly, both from country to country and within individual countries themselves. In the Netherlands East Indies, for example, the Japanese invaders were welcomed almost as liberators, and a local nationalist group was eventually to be invested with domestic power by the conquerers as a proto-independent government. In Norway, which fought bitterly against overwhelming odds in 1940, the Germans erected a puppet government of Norwegian Nazis, only to see it spurned by the majority of the population who went on to support one of the most effective European resistance movements. The behaviour of the occupied more commonly fell between these two ends of the spectrum.

Their behaviour was influenced by many factors, among which the strength of national feeling, cultural unity, and profundity of democratic tradition were the most important. It was also influenced, however, by German occupation policy. As Werner Rings had pointed out, there was no stereotyped German method; he counts seven, ranging from full military government — in northern France, Belgium, Serbia, Greece, and the eastern Ukraine — to control by the German Foreign Office in Denmark, where democratic elections were held as late as 1943.[1] Other countries were incorporated into the Reich, partitioned, or ruled as colonies. Poland, for example, was partitioned, parts of it being incorporated into the Reich, parts governed by a governor general responsible to Hitler, parts ruled as colonies under Reich commissars.

The occupied collaborated, acquiesced, or resisted in equal variety. In Holland, after the flight of the Queen and her ministers to London in May 1940, government was carried on, under pre-war provisions, by the senior civil servants of the ministries, answering to a Reich commissar; the population was strongly hostile to the occupation authority, but armed resistance was not an option in a densely populated and urban country. There was a strong Dutch Nazi party, despised by the patriot majority, and tens of thousands of young Dutchmen volunteered for the Waffen SS.[2] Holland's worst ordeal came at the very end of the war, when its transformation into a battleground interrupted agricultural supply, leading to semi-starvation in the great cities.[3]

In Denmark, favourably treated by Germany as a brother Aryan society, the invasion of April 9, 1940, scarcely interrupted the country's normal life. The defences were overwhelmed with little loss of life; the King remained on his throne and his government continued in office. Danish patriots supplied intelligence to London and undertook sabotage, but the country was too easily controlled for effective resistance to develop; some Danes volunteered for the Waffen SS.[4] On the other hand, when the occupiers attempted to implement the Final Solution policy in 1943, the popular will impeded their actions, and the whole Jewish community of seven thousand was spirited away into neutral Sweden.[5]

Norway had had a small Nazi party from before the war, led by an embittered ex-minister Vidkun Quisling; his name was to be taken into universal use for that of the collaborator. Appointing himself head of government on April 9, 1940, he was subsequently removed from office by the Germans and not reappointed until 1942. Nevertheless, he and his subordinates served the Nazis loyally to the end, in a country which, though it yielded some Waffen SS volunteers, provided the SOE with its most dependable and spirited supporters in Western Europe. Among their many achievements was to set back the German nuclear weapons program by many months.[6]

In Belgium, occupation took the form, as it had done during the First World War, of direct military government. The reason, in both cases, was to ensure the closest possible integration of the country's coal, iron, and steel production with Germany's; the arrangement underlay those voluntarily formalized in the postwar Coal and Steel Community. There was little resistance to occupation in Belgium; though the military administration was unpopular, government was carried on, as in Holland, by senior civil servants. On the other hand, to an even greater extent than in Holland, Belgium produced active and enthusiastic collaborators with the Nazi regime. The Rexist movement, originally a right-wing Catholic group, took on Nazi trappings, preached a Nazi message of national regeneration, and provided large numbers of volunteers to the Waffen SS. Its leader, Léon Degrelle, became a favourite of Hitler and won the highest German decorations for bravery. He succeeded in escaping from the battle of Berlin in April 1945 to find refuge in Spain.[7]

Spain, a skilful neutral throughout the Second World War, whose leader, Franco, parlayed successfully with both the Allies and the Axis, was nevertheless indirectly involved through the despatch of a volunteer division, the Division Azul, to fight with the Germans against Bolshevism on the Eastern Front.[8]

Franco's skill lay in subordinating his ideological sympathy with the Nazi system to his sense of Spanish national interest. He hedged his bets against the likelihood of German victory and of Allied defence, both of which

seemed strong in 1940–41. Mussolini, by contrast, made
the mistake of committing himself wholeheartedly to
Germany, largely through his personal desire to stand as
an equal to Hitler, his junior — and initial imitator — in
the business of dictatorship. Emulation was a disaster for
Italy. It led to its humiliation by the Greeks in the winter
of 1940, by the British in Libya in early 1941, and in East
Africa later that year. In the wake of the German defeat of
Yugoslavia and Greece, Italy occupied much of those two
countries, as it had southeastern France after its inglori-
ous attempt at invasion in June 1940. Its involvement in
Hitler's imperial policies only weakened its forces by dispersion. When the Allies struck at Sicily in August 1943,
and then at the mainland in September, Italian military
resistance collapsed. Mussolini became a refugee in his
own country, first rescued from captivity, then installed as
a puppet head of a shrunken state by German power. His
relationship with Hitler indeed showed itself to be brutally one-sided in essence.[9] The consequences for his fellow
countrymen of his rise and fall have been arrestingly narrated by Richard Lamb.[10] A more ambiguous element of
the story of Italy's involvement in the war concerns the
role of the papacy. Pius XII, a good man but weak Pope,
declined to confront his worldwide flock with a denunciation of Hitler's crimes lest he provoke the German occupiers of Italy into violating the Vatican's immunity. His
decision to stand above the great moral issues of the
Second World War compromised papal authority for
much of the postwar period.[11]

The most complex of relationships between Germany and an occupied country unrolled in France, its chief historic enemy. The occupation arrangements were complex in themselves. Until November 1942, when the Anglo-American invasion of French North Africa terminated the exemption, the southern-central zone of France remained unoccupied by the German troops who had overwhelmed the French army in June 1940. By the terms of the 1940 armistice, French sovereignty remained intact, absolute in the unoccupied "Vichy" zone, mediated in northern France and the eastern and western borders by the presence of the Wehrmacht. Vichy was the legitimate inheritor of the powers of the Third Republic, and Pétain a constitutional head of state.[12] Almost all Frenchmen gave Pétain their loyalty; those who followed de Gaulle into "Free France" were both a tiny minority — only 7,000 of the 195,000 French soldiers evacuated from Dunkirk volunteered for him — and legally in mutiny.[13] Until June 22, 1942, those technically loyal to Vichy also included the members of the French Communist party, which, Russian alliance of August 1939 as its official line throughout the Phoney War.

After Hitler's attack on Russia, the party at once took up hostility to the regime and began to organize what would prove the most effective branch of the resistance. The resistance was, however, many things, representing all shades of political opinion in France except those of the extreme right. There were socialist, military-traditionalist, Catholic, and Gaullist movements which, from 1943 onwards, de Gaulle tried to bring under a central organization. Such a body, Le Conseil national de la résistance (CNR) was, with difficulty, set up; the communists in particular kept their options open and their powder dry. During 1943, the resistance gained greatly in numbers as a result of the German introduction of labour conscription in France; not until 1944, however, did the Maquis, as the various armed groups were collectively known, embark on widespread military action.[14] It proved a nuisance rather than an impediment to German operations; at Vercors and Glières, where the Maquis attempted to create "liberated areas," the Wehrmacht reacted with savagery, obliterating resistance and massacring the survivors.[15] Great honour is due to all who actively resisted in France; their armed numbers have been estimated at about 116,000 by June 6, 1944. They ran terrible risks and were savagely punished whenever they fell into German hands. The truth is, however, that their numbers were greatly exceeded by those who prudently held aloof from opposing the occupation, the vast majority, and probably by those who collaborated.

Collaboration took many forms. Commercial collaboration was common; industrialists had to make a living, and Germany offered markets, even if payment was made in overpriced occupation marks; informing, to curry favour or settle scores, was also common; outright collaboration, as propagandist or security policeman, was the least common, but several hundred thousand

Frenchmen nevertheless took that route. Many who collaborated paid the price in the immediate aftermath of liberation. There were hundreds, perhaps thousands, of summary executions, often carried out by the communist Maquis. On the other hand, some of the most highly placed collaborators talked their way out of trouble or suffered merely formal punishment.[17] Pétain, the symbol of the ambiguity of French relations with Germany in the Vichy years, was condemned to death, but the sentence was commuted and he was incarcerated for the rest of his life in the island fortress of the Ile d'Yeu.

Resistance in Western Europe, though it sustained national pride, harmed the German occupation forces little. In Eastern Europe, it caused the occupiers considerable trouble, ranging in scale from chronic insecurity to outright civil war. The explanation for that lies chiefly in the harshness of German policy in the Slav lands but also in local traditions of resistance to alien authority. In Greece, the only non-Slav country of the region to be conquered and occupied, memories of the war of independence against the Ottomans remained strong. There was also a more recent, home-grown Communist party deeply rooted in peasant hostility to landlords and government. The British, through the SOE, helped to revive the tradition of resistance, which was inflamed by German disruption of the economy, leading to famine in the winter of 1941. By 1943, disorder was widespread and heightened by conflict between left and right within the guerrilla movement. Something like civil war broke out, to which the Germans responded with atrocity and massacre. Hunger killed 40,000 Greeks; German reprisals, another 25,000; the civil war, ended only by British intervention at Christmas 1944, uncounted numbers.[18]

In Yugoslavia, already surveyed as a theatre of campaign in its own right, resistance to foreign occupation — by Bulgaria and Hungary, as well as Italy and Germany — was immediate, and soon intense. Mihailovic, the chief Serb resistant, sought to delay a general uprising, the Ustanka, until the prospect of outside assistance made success realistic. Tito, the communist leader, insisted, after the German attack in Russia, on raising and spreading rebellion as widely as possible. As the Croats and, to some extent, the Muslims of Bosnia preferred the occupiers to the old Serb-dominated royal government, the brutalities of civil war were soon added to those of occupation. With British assistance, Tito was eventually to prevail, in a terrible internal war that cost the lives of 1.6 million Yugoslavs, one-tenth of the pre-war population. The account written by the head of the British military mission to Tito, Fitzroy Maclean, remains, though partial, indispensable.[19]

In Poland, the policy of the principal resistance organization, the Home Army, was also to delay rebellion against the German occupiers until victory was a realistic probability. Poland had a long tradition of resistance to foreign conquerors, and national solidarity was strong. The existence of a legitimate government in exile and of a strong army abroad — Poland, even in 1944, had the fourth-largest number of men fighting Germany, after the Soviet Union, the United States, and the United Kingdom lent powerful heart to the Poles, who produced few collaborators and no puppet chief, a unique distinction in the record of European response to German aggression.[20] In the aftermath of Operation Bagration, however, the Russian offensive which destroyed the German Army Group Centre in July 1944, the Polish high command decided to unleash the long-prepared rebellion by seizing the city of Warsaw, in order to pre-empt its liberation by the Russians and re-establish patriotic government there.[21] It had reckoned without the duplicity of Stalin, who halted the Red Army's advance within sound of the firing in Warsaw until the Germans had crushed the Home Army.

Guerrillas in the Soviet Union played an altogether different role from that of the Chetniks and the Polish Home Army, attacking the rear of the Wehrmacht from early after the invasion. Regarded at first with suspicion by the Soviet high command, since they operated outside the chain of authority, they were soon seen to be valuable collaborators and were sent regular officers to act as advisers and leaders. Their principal zone of operations was the Pripet Marshes, which offered base areas that the Germans found difficulty in identifying and destroying. Anti-guerrilla campaigns caused a significant drain in German manpower and were much disliked by the ordinary soldiers, since it was a duty commonly visited on units withdrawn from the main fronts for "rest."

That was one of the reasons for the extreme brutality with which they were conducted. When the Germans were able to surround guerrilla groups, which often contained families as well as fighters, they killed everyone over whom they gained power.[22] On the other hand, even during preliminaries to Operation Bagration, the partisans never succeeded in interrupting the Wehrmacht's logistical organization or in impeding a German retreat.[23] As victory approached, the high command progressively withdrew its support from the partisans and directed personnel recuperated from behind the lines to regular assault units, which had low survival prospects; partisan officers were often demoted in rank. The guerrilla spirit was not welcomed by the Stalinist dictatorship.

This does not exhaust the record of European resistance to occupation and dictatorship. The SOE, for example, also supported resistance movements in Albania, Bulgaria, Hungary, and Romania, though the last three countries had been diplomatically aligned with Germany for much of the war. Czechoslovakia was a prime source of intelligence to the Allies; the puppet Slovak state staged its own rising against the Germans in 1944, in anticipation of Soviet intervention, which was put down with terrible severity. It has become fashionable in recent years to speak of a German "resistance" to Hitler, predicated in the undoubted existence of an internal opposition which revealed itself to the outside world through the Bomb Plot of July 20, 1944. The plot has generated an enormous literature — justifiably so, for it was one of the most dramatic events of the Second World War. There have been numerous biographies of the principal conspirators, including J. Kramarz's of Claus von Stauffenberg and G. MacDonagh's of Adam von Trott.[24] The difficulty in recognizing a true German "resistance" lies in the aims, rather than the motives, of the conspirators.[25] Trott and Stauffenberg were genuinely disgusted by the Nazis and outraged by the abasement of Germany's good name that Nazi atrocities had brought about. Nevertheless, they failed to understand the determination of Germany's enemies to break its power and continued to hope, up to the moment when Stauffenberg planted the bomb under Hitler's table, that the "good" Germans could persuade the Western allies to grant it a separate peace, so allowing it to extricate itself from defeat by Russia.[26] Against any such attempt at dividing the alliance, the British and Americans adamantly set their face. Apologists for the opponents of Hitler have attempted to argue that a chance of shortening the war was missed by the Western refusal to treat with Trott and his collaborators; such apologies overlook both the depth of anti-German feeling that understandably possessed Western populations and the strength of popular solidarity, equally understandable, with Soviet Russia that complemented it.

The Germany of the Nazi years remains an incomprehensible phenomenon to Western consciousness. Two books widely read in the West which unveil something of its mystery are Christabel Bieienberg's *The Past Is Myself* and Missie Vassiltchikov's *Berlin Diaries*. It is significant that both are the work of women; femininity was deliberately devalued in the Nazi system; it is also significant that both were foreigners involuntarily trapped within wartime Germany as semi-detached observers of its tensions and follies.[27]

Apart from the testimony of internees and prisoners of war, we lack any comparable picture from the inside of the nature of the Japanese occupation of China and East Asia. The relationship between the Japanese and the indigenous peoples of the European colonies was an ambivalent one. As fellow Asians, they had inflicted a humiliation on the whites which would preclude any lasting reimposition of colonial rule in the East Indies, Burma, and Malaya after the war. Even as fellow Asians, however, they eventually succeeded in making themselves unpopular with all but a handful of puppets; they formed close relationships with nationalist élites in several countries, particularly Burma and the future Indonesia, but the motives of such élites were patriotic, not self-serving.[28] Their greatest success in subverting the war effort of their enemies was the formation of the Indian National Army from prisoners of war taken from the British-Indian Army at the hall of Singapore. Though a failure as a military force, it contributed by its mere existence to the undermining of British authority in India and so to the acceleration of the granting of independence in 1947.[29] Christopher Thorne supplies the best survey of

Japan's relations with the peoples of the conquered areas in *The Far Eastern War*.[30]

The Japanese were harsh occupiers, and worse than harsh with the European prisoners who fell into their hands. Their cruelties were, however, pragmatic and unsystematized. In Europe, the Germans behaved quite differently. They had a policy of oppression and exploitation against "inferior" peoples, and of genocide against the Jews. Omer Bartov has argued that the German army committed systematic atrocities against the Russians from the outset of Operation Barbarossa, a charge not accepted by all historians.[31] The role of the SS, the armed wing of the Nazi party, is undisputed. It was an instrument of terror against all opponents of the regime, outside and inside Germany, where it set up the first concentration camps in 1934. From January 1942, it also became the agent of the "Final Solution," the plans to exterminate all Jews with the German area of control. During 1942, the SS sent "special commandos" into the recently captured areas of the Soviet Union and Baltic states where centres of Jewish settlement had thrived since the Middle Ages and began to massacre their inhabitants by shooting. Massacre soon gave way to organized gassing at extermination camps set up in remote areas of southern and eastern Poland, including Auschwitz, Sobibor, and Treblinka.[32] The earliest victims were found close to hand. As their numbers dwindled, the SS cast its net wider, concentrating the Jews of the outlying conquered areas, including Western, and then Southern,

Europe, into transportation centres and sending them by rail to the camps for destruction. Meanwhile, the SS was also becoming a power within the Nazi system in its own right, operating factories staffed by forced labour which was worked to debility and death; it was also taking over the control of the police, security, and intelligence apparatuses within the Nazi empire. By the end, the SS constituted a state within a state, unfettered by law and menacing the autonomy of all other institutions in Germany.[33]

The SS tarnished the name of Germany, perhaps in perpetuity. The stain of guilt certainly remains to this day. Germany's crimes determined the Allies to undertake an unprecedented measure of retribution, the convening of an international tribunal to try its leaders for offences not only against international law but also against humanity. The leading criminals — Hitler, Goebbels, Himmler — escaped punishment by taking their own lives, the last as a prisoner in British hands; others, including Heydrich, Himmler's principal lieutenant, had already been killed or else, like Bormann, Hitler's personal functionary, had disappeared in the last days of the fighting in Berlin. Enough survived, however, to fill the dock at Nuremberg with several rows of accused, including Hess, once Hitler's deputy; Göring, his heir presumptive; Dönitz, the last Nazi head of state; Streicher, Nazism's leading anti-Semite; Frank, governor general of Poland; Sauckel, the director of forced labour; Kaltenbrunner, head of the SS security police; Ribbentrop, Hitler's foreign minister; and

Speer, the director of German war industry. Some of the accused were found not guilty; some were convicted but sentenced to imprisonment. The most prominent of those convicted were hanged; Göring escaped the gallows by committing suicide on the eve of execution. A major account of the Nuremberg trials is provided by Ann Tusa and John Tusa.[34] A compelling eye-witness narrative of the courtroom drama and of the prisoners' reactions to their examination and fates was written by the principal psychiatrist, an American, who succeeds brilliantly in presenting his subjects as human beings without deviating from the repulsion their crimes produce. This now largely forgotten book is one of the most compelling documents of the Second World War.[35]

"A thousand years will pass and the guilt of Germany will not be erased," confessed Frank during the trial. It is an unchallengeable verdict on the war. As the condemned awaited execution, the Allies struggled to cope with the human disaster of the war's aftermath. At the height of his power, Hitler had controlled territory inhabited by 260 million people, twice more than the population of the United States. He had been the direct cause of the deaths — among Germans, the occupied, and his opponents — of at least twenty million, and indirectly of as many as thirty million more. The Germans of the Reich and of the German settlements in Eastern Europe had paid a terrible price for his determination to avenge the defeat of 1918. Four million Reich citizens had been killed; seventeen million Germans settled for centuries in Eastern Europe had been driven from their homes in 1945–46, of whom at least three million died in the exodus.[36] Germany, once the most populous and powerful state in Central Europe, was divided, occupied, bankrupt, and inert.[37] It was to be rescued from hunger and desolation only by the generosity of its enemies.

No six years of history have been more written about than 1939–45. This selection of books scarcely indicates the scale of historical effort to record and analyze the events of that period. They are those which one historian has found an indispensable guide to the war's drama and tragedy.

NOTES

CHAPTER ONE

1. A.J.P. Taylor, *The Origins of the Second World War* (New York, 1962).

CHAPTER TWO

1. James McPherson, *Battle Cry of Freedom: The Civil War Era* (New York, 1988).
2. Chester Wilmot, *The Struggle for Europe* (London, 1951).
3. International Military Tribunal, *Trial of the Major War Criminals*, 42 vols. (Nuremberg, 1946–49); *U.S. Strategic Bombing Survey* (Washington, D.C., 1945 ff.); W.S. Churchill, *The Second World War*, 6 vols. (London, 1948–54).

4. Guy Wint and Peter Calvocoressi, *Total War*, rev. 2d ed. (London, 1989).

5. Gerhard L. Weinberg, *A World at Arms* (Cambridge, 1994).

6. Martin Gilbert, *Second World War* (London, 1989).

7. Militärgeschichtlicheforschungsamt, Freiburg im Breisgau, *Das Deutsche Reich undder Zweite Weltkrieg* (in progress).

8. M.M. Postan, D. Hay, and J.D. Scott, *Design and Development of Weapons* (London, 1964).

9. Captain S.W. Roskill, *The War at Sea*, 3 vols. (London, 1961); Sir Charles Webster and Noble Frankland, *The Strategic Air Offensive Against Germany*, 4 vols. (London, 1961–65).

10. G. Harrison, *Cross-Channel Attack* (Washington, D.C., 1951).

11. (Washington, D.C., 1951–73); F.C. Pogue, *The Supreme Command* (Washington, D.C., 1954).

12. (Bloomington, Ind., 1981).

13. W. Craven and J. Cate, *The Army Air Forces in World War II*, 7 vols. (Chicago, 1948–58).

14. S.E. Morison, *United States Naval Operations in World War II*, 15 vols. (Boston, 1947–62).

15. John Erickson, *The Road to Stalingrad* (London, 1975), and *The Road to Berlin* (London, 1983).

16. A Dallin, *German Rule in Russia* (London, 1957).

17. Joan Beaumont, *Comrades in Arms* (London, 1980).

18. Alan S. Milward, *The German Economy at War* (London, 1965).

19. H. Trevor-Roper, *Hitler's War Directives, 1939–45* (London, 1964).

20. P. Scramm et al., *Kriegstagebuch des Oberkommandos der Wehrmacht*, 4 vols. in 7 parts (Frankfurt-am-Main, 1961–65).

21. W. Warlimont, *Inside Hitler's Headquarters*, trans. by R.H. Barry (London, 1964).
22. R. Storrey, *A History of Modern Japan* (London, 1960), and *The Double Patriots* (Boston, 1957).
23. R. Spector, *Eagle Against the Sun* (New York, 1988).
24. H.P. Willmott, *Empires in the Balance* (Annapolis, 1982), and *The Barrier and the Javelin* (Annapolis, 1983).
25. Donald Cameron Watt, *How War Came* (London, 1989).

CHAPTER THREE

1. W.S. Churchill, *The Second World War*, 6 vols. (London, 1948–54); Charles de Gaulle, *The War Memoirs* (New York, 1955).
2. David Irving, *Hitler's War* (London, 1977).
3. Martin Gilbert, *Finest Hour* (London, 1983) and *Road to Victory* (London, 1986).
4. James McGregor Burns, *Roosevelt: The Soldier of Freedom* (New York, 1970).
5. Forrest C. Pogue, *George C. Marshall: Order and Hope, 1939–42* (New York, 1965) and *Organizer of Victory, 1943–45* (New York, 1973).
6. John Erickson, *The Road to Stalingrad* (London, 1975).
7. Allan Bullock, *Hitler and Stalin* (London, 1991).
8. V.I. Chuikov, *The Beginning of the Road* (London, 1963).
9. Alvin Cox, *Tojo* (New York, 1975).
10. C. Barnett, ed., *Hitler's Generals* (London, 1989); J. Keegan, ed., *Churchill's Generals* (London, 1991); Harold Shukman, ed., *Stalin's Generals* (London, 1993).
11. Desmond Young, *Rommel* (London, 1950).
12. Erich von Manstein, *Lost Victories* (London, 1958).
13. Heinz Guderian, *Panzer Leader* (London, 1952).
14. David Irving, *Göring* (London, 1989).

15. Peter Padfield, *Dönitz: The Last Führer* (London, 1970).
16. Albert Speer, *Inside the Third Reich* (London, 1970).
17. H. Trevor-Roper, *The Last Days of Hitler*, 2d ed. (London, 1950).
18. Nigel Hamilton, *Montgomery*, 3 vols. (London, 1981–86).
19. Correlli Barnett, *The Desert Generals*, 2d ed. (London, 1983).
20. Nigel Nicolson, *Alex* (London, 1973).
21. Stephen Ambrose, *Eisenhower*, Vol. 1 (London, 1984).
22. E.B. Sledge, *With the Old Breed* (Novato, Calif., 1981).
23. M. Djilas, *Wartime* (New York, 1977).
24. George MacDonald Fraser, *Quartered Safe Out Here* (London, 1992).
25. Alvin Kernan, *Crossing the Line* (Annapolis, 1994).
26. Alexander Stahlberg, *Bounden Duty* (London, 1990).
27. James Jones, *The Thin Red Line* (New York, 1962).
28. Evelyn Waugh, *Men at Arms* (London, 1952); *Officers and Gentlemen* (London, 1955); *Unconditional Surrender* (London, 1961).

CHAPTER FOUR

1. Robert M. Kennedy, *The German Campaign in Poland* (Washington, D.C., 1956); Nicholas Bethell, *The War Hitler Won: The Fall of Poland, September 1939* (London, 1972).
2. Thomas Rics, *Cold Will: The Defence of Finland* (London, 1988).
3. François Kersaudy, *Norway, 1940* (London, 1990).
4. Alistair Horne, *To Lose a Battle* (London, 1969); J. Benoist-Méchin, *Sixty Days that Shook the West* (London, 1956).
5. Brian Bond, *France and Belgium, 1939–40* (London, 1983);

L.F. Ellis, *The War in France and Flanders* (London, 1953).

6. Marc Block, *Strange Defeat* (Oxford, 1949).
7. Telford Taylor, *The Breaking Wave* (London, 1967).
8. Williamson Murray, *Luftwaffe* (London, 1985).
9. Michael Howard, *The Mediterranean Strategy in the Second World War* (London, 1968).
10. C. Barnett, *The Desert Generals*, 2d ed. (London, 1983); Anthony Mocker, *Haile Selassie's War* (Oxford, 1984).
11. Anthony Beevor, *Crete: The Battle and the Resistance* (London, 1991); Alan Clarke, *The Battle of Crete* (London, 1962); I. Stewart, *The Struggle for Crete* (Oxford, 1966).
12. Graf von der Heydte, *Daedalus Returned* (London, 1958).
13. Fitzroy Maclean, *Disputed Barricades* (London, 1957); William Deakin, *The Embattled Mountain* (London, 1971); Franklin Lindsay, *Beacons in the Night* (Stamford, 1993).
14. Martin Van Crefeld, *Hitler's Strategy, 1940–41: The Balkan Clue* (London, 1973).
15. Alan Clark, *Barbarossa* (London, 1965).
16. L. Goure, *The Siege of Leningrad* (New York, 1971).
17. V.I. Chuikov, *The Beginning of the Road* (London, 1963); Geoffrey Jukes, *Hitler's Stalingrad Decisions* (Berkeley, 1985).
18. Geoffrey Jukes, *Kursk: The Clash of Armour* (London, 1968).
19. Gerd Niepold, *Mittlere Ostfront Juni, 1944* (Herford, 1985).
20. J.K. Zawodny, *Nothing But Honour: The Story of the Warsaw Uprising, 1944* (London, 1978).
21. Christopher Duffy, *Red Storm on the Reich* (New York, 1991).
22. Cornelius Ryan, *The Last Battle* (London, 1966).

23. A.B. Gaunson, *The Anglo-French Clash in Syria and Lebanon* (London, 1987).
24. Barrie Pitt, *The Crucible of War* (London, 1980).
25. Jonathan Steinberg, *All or Nothing: The Axis and the Holocaust* (London, 1990).
26. Shelford Bidwell and Dominick Graham, *Tug of War: The Battle for Italy, 1943–45* (New York, 1986).
27. Jeffrey Holland, *The Aegean Mission* (New York, 1988).
28. Chester Wilmot, *The Struggle for Europe* (London, 1951); Max Hastings, *Overlord* (New York, 1984); Carlo d'Este, *Decision in Normandy* (London, 1983); Alexander McKee, *Caen* (London, 1964); John Keegan, *Six Armies in Normandy* (London, 1982).
29. Robert Kershaw, *It Never Snows in September* (London, 1990).
30. Milton Shulman, *Defeat in the West* (London, 1947).
31. John Eisenhower, *The Bitter Woods* (Toronto, 1969).
32. Richard Wilson, *When Tigers Fight* (New York, 1983).
33. Gordon Prang, *At Dawn We Slept* (New York, 1981).
34. Samuel Eliot Morison, *Coral Sea, Midway and Submarine Operations* (Boston, 1949).
35. Richard Grenfell, *Main Fleet to Singapore* (London, 1951).
36. Louis Allen, *Burma: The Longest War* (London, 1984).
37. William Slim, *Defeat into Victory* (London, 1956); John Masters, *The Road Past Mandalay* (New York, 1961).
38. William Manchester, *American Caesar* (Boston 1978); J.D. Potter, *Nimitz* (Annapolis, 1976).
39. H. Cannon, *Leyte* (Washington, D.C., 1954); S. Falk, *Decision at Leyte* (New York, 1966); R.R. Smith, *Triumph in the Philippines* (Washington, D.C., 1953).
40. R. Appelman et al., *Okinawa, the Last Battle* (Washington, D.C., 1948).
41. H. Feis, *Japan Subdued* (Princeton, 1961); J.F.C. Butow,

Japan's Decision to Surrender (Stanford, 1954).

42. David Glantz, *August Storm* (Fort Leavenworth, 1983).

43. Vincent J. Esposits, ed., *The West Point Atlas of American Wars*, Vol. 2 (New York, 1959).

44. J. Keegan, ed., *The Times Atlas of the Second World War* (London, 1989).

CHAPTER FIVE

1. F.W. Winterbotham, *The Ultra Secret* (London, 1974).

2. F.H. Hinsley et al., *British Intelligence in the Second World War*, 4 vols. (London, 1979–90).

3. F.H. Hinsley and Alan Stripp, *The Codebreakers* (Oxford, 1993).

4. Bradley Smith, *The Ultra–Magic Deals* (London, 1993).

5. Ronald Lewin, *The American Magic: Codes, Ciphers and the Defeat of Japan* (New York, 1982).

6. Gordon Welchman, *The Hut Six Story* (London, 1982).

7. Andrew Hodges, *Alan Turing* (London, 1983).

8. W. Kozaczuk, *Enigma* (London, 1984).

9. R. Bennett, *Ultra in the West* (London, 1979).

10. R. Bennett, *Ultra and Mediterranean Strategy* (London, 1989).

11. P. Beesly, *Very Special Intelligence* (London, 1977).

12. D. Kahn, *Seizing the Enigma* (London, 1991).

13. C. Andrew, *Secret Service* (London, 1985).

14. F.W. Deakin and G.R. Storrey, *The Case of Richard Sorge* (London, 1966).

15. J.C. Masterman, *The Double Cross System* (London, 1973).

16. M.R.D. Foot, *SOE* (London, 1984).

17. M.R.D. Foot, *SOE in France* (London, 1966).

18. J. Ganlinski, *Poland, SOE and the Allies* (London, 1969).

19. J.G. Beevor, *SOE* (London, 1981).

20. F.W. Deakin, *The Embattled Mountain* (Oxford, 1971).
21. M. Lees, *The Rape of Serbia* (New York, 1990).
22. Franklin Lindsay, *Beacons in the Night* (Stanford, 1993).
23. A. Milward, *The German Economy at War* (London, 1965).
24. A. Milward, *The New Order and the French Economy* (Oxford, 1970) and *The Fascist Economy in Norway* (Oxford, 1972).
25. A. Milward, *War, Economy and Society, 1939–45* (London, 1977).
26. Studs Terkel, *"The Good War": An Oral History of World War Two* (London, 1955), p. 573.
27. T.A. Bisson, *Zaibitsu Control and Foreign Policy in Japan* (Berkeley, 1954); W. Carr, *Arms, Autarky and Aggression* (London, 1972).
28. F.C. Jones, *Japan's New Order in East Asia* (London, 1954).
29. G. Fuà, *Notes on Italian Economic Growth* (Milan, 1965).
30. C. Behrens, *Merchant Shipping and the Demands of War* (London, 1955).
31. U.S. Civilian Production Administration, *Industrial Mobilization for War* (Washington, D.C., 1947).
32. Milward, *War, Economy and Society*, pp. 156, 163.
33. Milward, *The Fascist Economy in Norway*.
34. M. Gowing, *Britain and Atomic Energy, 1939–45* (London, 1964).
35. N. Longmate, Hitler's Rockets (London, 1985).

CHAPTER SIX

1. Werner Rings, *Living with the Enemy* (London, 1982).
2. W. Warmbrunn, *The Dutch under German Occupation* (Stanford, 1983).
3. H. Zee, *The Hunger Winter* (London, 1982).
4. C. Cruikshank, *SOE in Scandinavia* (Oxford, 1986);

D. Lampe, *The Savage Canary* (London, 1957).

5. L. Goldberger, ed., *The Rescue of the Danish Jews* (New York, 1987).

6. P. Hayes, *The Career and Political Ideas of Vidkin Quisling* (Newton Abbot, 1971).

7. M. Conway, *Collaboration in Belgium* (New Haven, 1993).

8. G. Klenfeld and G. Tambs, *Hitler's Spanish Legion* (Carbondale, 1979).

9. F.W. Deakin, *The Brutal Friendship* (New York, 1966).

10. R. Lamb, *War in Italy: A Brutal Story* (London, 1993).

11. S. Friedlander, *Pius XII and the Third Reich* (New York, 1966).

12. R. Aron, *The Vichy Regime* (London, 1958).

13. François Kersaudy, *Churchill and de Gaulle* (London, 1981).

14. H.R. Kedward, *In Search of the Maquis* (Oxford, 1993).

15. L. Jourdan et al., *Glières* (Annécy, 1946).

16. M. Dank, *The French Against the French* (Philadelphia, 1974); G. Hirschfeld and P. Marsh, *Collaboration in France* (Oxford, 1989).

17. A. Beevor and A. Cooper, *Paris after the Liberation* (London, 1994).

18. Mark Mazower, *Inside Hitler's Greece* (New Haven, 1993).

19. Fitzroy Maclean, *Disputed Barricades* (London, 1957).

20. J.T. Gross, *Polish Society under German Occupation* (Princeton, 1979).

21. G. Bruce, *The Warsaw Uprising* (London, 1979).

22. J. Armstrong, ed., *Soviet Partisans in World War II* (Madison, 1956).

23. E. Howell, *The Soviet Partisan Movement* (Washington, D.C., 1956).

24. G. MacDonagh, *A Good German: Adam von Trott zu Solz* (London, 1989); C. Sykes, *Troubled Loyalties*

(London, 1956); J. Kramarz, *Stauffenberg* (London, 1967).

25. H. Rothfels, *The German Opposition to Hitler* (London, 1961).

26. F. Carston, *The German Resistance to Hitler* (London, 1970).

27. C. Bielenberg, *The Past Is Myself* (London, 1968); M. Vassiltchikov, *Berlin Diaries* (London, 1985).

28. W. Elsbree, *Japan's Role in Southeast Asian Nationalist Movements* (Cambridge, Mass., 1953); J. Lebra, *Japanese-Trained Armies in Southeast Asia* (New York, 1977).

29. H. Toye, *The Springing Tiger* (London, 1959).

30. C. Thorne, *The Far Eastern War, States and Societies* (London, 1986).

31. O. Bartov, *The Eastern Front* (London, 1985).

32. G. Reutlinger, *The Final Solution* (London, 1953).

33. H. Buchheim et al., *The Anatomy of the SS State* (London, 1968).

34. A. Tusa and J. Tusa, *The Nuremberg Trials* (London, 1963).

35. G. Gilbert, *Nuremberg Diary* (London, 1963).

36. M. Marrus and A. Bramwell, *Refugees in the Age of Total War* (London, 1968).

37. T. Sharp, *The Wartime Alliance and the Zonal Division of Germany* (Oxford, 1975).